THE
RESISTANCE SOLUTION

Why Educators Resist Change and What They Need Instead

BECCA SILVER

ISBN paperback 978-1-965438-17-6
ISBN ebook 978-1-965438-18-3

Published by Soro Publishing

For more information about our books and authors,
visit our website: www.soropublishing.com.

Table of Contents

Foreword

Steve Barkley

Instructional coaches and school leaders quickly learn that resistance rarely announces itself loudly. More often, it appears in small moments—a hesitant response during a meeting, a polite nod that doesn't lead to classroom change, a question that carries more of a statement than curiosity. When these moments occur, it is easy to interpret them as reluctance, disagreement, or even opposition. Yet the most effective leaders come to recognize that resistance is rarely the real problem. Resistance is information.

Very early in my work as a teacher leader, I participated in a verbal skills training program that introduced an idea I've carried with me ever since: resistance usually comes from somewhere. Sometimes it grows out of emotion, sometimes from pride or professional identity, and sometimes from intellectual disagreement. The training suggested that our response should match the source—empathy for emotion, approval for identity, and support for reasoning. I came to understand that we cannot change another person's thinking for them. What we can do is create conditions in which people feel safe enough, capable enough, and respected enough to examine their own thinking and consider new possibilities.

Over time, that early learning shaped my work with instructional coaches and school leaders. When resistance is taken personally, defensiveness emerges—and collaboration and change become highly unlikely. When coaches hear resistance, my advice has long been to respond with questions and paraphrasing rather than telling. Responding with curiosity instead of defensiveness keeps conversations open and maintains relationships—both essential conditions for meaningful growth.

Becca Silver's work extended my insights in powerful and practical ways. We have had several engaging podcast conversations where she reinforced listening even more carefully. Listening—not just for where resistance comes from, but for what it may be protecting and what someone needs next. Her framework shifts resistance from something leaders must manage to something leaders can interpret. Resistance stops sounding like opposition and begins sounding like information.

At times when leaders experience resistance they push harder or tighten expectations. At other times, they worry that pressing forward will damage relationships they value. The tension between maintaining humanity and maintaining expectations is one of the most difficult aspects of leadership in schools. This book offers another way to navigate that tension. Rather than asking leaders to choose between support and accountability, Becca shows how understanding what sits underneath resistance allows both to exist together.

One of the important contributions of this book is how clearly it names the questions educators are often asking themselves when change is introduced: Does this matter? Can I succeed? Do I belong in this work? Is growth possible here? Can I influence what happens next?

When those questions remain unanswered, resistance naturally follows. When leaders learn to listen for these questions, their responses begin to change. Conversations become more about understanding than about convincing. Progress becomes less about compliance and more about commitment.

After years of working alongside coaches and administrators responding to resistance, I found my own listening sharpened by Becca's perspective. Her work helped me recognize more clearly that resistance is something to learn from. When coaches respond to resistance with thoughtful questions and genuine curiosity, they and the coachee uncover the information needed to support real change. This reinforced my long-held coaching stance of serving as a thought partner.

As you read this book, you will likely begin recognizing familiar moments from your own work—conversations that stalled, initiatives that lost traction, or classrooms where change felt slower than you hoped. Becca's framework offers a way to revisit those moments with new insight and renewed possibilities. Instead of asking how to overcome resistance, you will begin asking what the resistance is telling you. Resistance stops being a barrier. It becomes an invitation to understand what people need next. That shift has the potential to transform not only individual conversations, but the culture of growth within a school.

Becca Silver has provided educators with a thoughtful and practical guide for making that shift. I believe you will find, as I did, that once you begin listening for what sits underneath resistance, your coaching and leadership conversations—and the change they support—begin to feel different in positive and important ways.

Introduction

You're standing at the front of the room during professional development, demonstrating for teachers a strategy you've been preparing to share for weeks. The research behind it matters. You believe it will help students learn more deeply if it actually makes its way into classrooms.

As you begin explaining the approach, something catches your attention out of the corner of your eye.

A teacher rolls their eyes.

The moment is quick, subtle enough that most people in the room probably don't notice. The teacher doesn't say anything. She sits quietly and jots a few notes, and the professional development session moves on as if nothing happened.

The moment lingers in your mind longer than it should.

As teachers gather their things and head out, you catch yourself replaying it. What did that eye roll mean? Frustration? Skepticism? Maybe exhaustion from one more initiative landing on an already full plate.

A few weeks later you step into that teacher's classroom and the strategy from the training is nowhere to be seen.

If you work as a coach or school leader, scenes like this probably feel familiar. Resistance shows up in ways that can be easy to miss: an eye roll, a hesitant comment, or a polite nod that never turns into action. Sometimes it's harder to ignore: a blunt pushback, a frustrated tone, or a flat-out refusal.

Getting adults to change in the moment is only part of the work. The real challenge is helping that change carry over once the meeting ends. What actually makes that happen comes down to human factors most of us were never taught to look for.

Those moments are where the real work starts.

Why This Work Feels Hard

Leading change in schools carries a kind of pressure that is easy to underestimate until you are the person responsible for moving the work forward.

For coaches, the pressure often feels personal. When teachers are slow to change, it can begin to feel like a reflection of the coach's influence. Doubt creeps in during moments that no one else sees.

Do the teachers take my role seriously?

Am I actually helping?

School and district leaders experience a different version of the pressure. When they're not seeing progress and a change isn't showing up in instruction, responsibility has a way of settling squarely on their shoulders. District expectations, improvement plans, and accountability measures loom in the background of every effort, shaping how success and failure are interpreted.

Initiatives that make little progress can feel like an ego hit.

All of these roles can also feel surprisingly lonely. Teachers bring frustrations and challenges to coaches and administrators, who are expected to project confidence even while navigating uncertainty themselves. Many people in these positions feel like they are supposed to have the answers while still searching for them.

Time only intensifies the pressure. Students need stronger instruction now, and district leaders want evidence that progress is happening. Accountability has raised the stakes. The pandemic left gaps that still need attention and district leaders want proof that progress is happening, often with fewer resources than before.

Coaches and administrators juggle classroom visits, meetings, professional learning, family communication, and countless small decisions that fill every corner of the day. The urgency of improvement pushes people toward action, even when the situation might benefit from a slower and more thoughtful approach.

Then there is the emotional whiplash that many leaders recognize immediately.

You leave a conversation feeling encouraged. A teacher seemed open, maybe even energized, and for a moment you allow yourself to believe that they are finally starting to make progress.

Then you walk into that same classroom and nothing has changed.

After enough experiences like this, expectations begin to shift almost without you noticing. Some leaders conclude that certain people are simply resistant to change. Others respond by applying more pressure, hoping stronger accountability will counter the resistance and keep things moving forward.

Neither reaction feels particularly satisfying, though both make sense when you consider the pressure leaders are under. The problem is… the resistance persists.

When the Problem Persists

Resistance rarely stays contained. It spreads through a school in ways that can be easy to miss at first.

As resistance persists, leaders often do what feels most responsible: they tighten accountability and add more structures to ensure follow-through. Walkthroughs become more frequent, checklists begin appearing in meetings, documentation grows, and conversations start revolving around whether expectations were met. The intention behind these moves is understandable. When progress feels fragile, pressure can seem like the most reliable way to keep it from slipping backward.

At the same time, coaches may begin questioning their effectiveness. Conversations circle back to the same challenges again and again, and the work that once felt energizing starts to feel exhausting.

Teachers feel it too. Some are being asked to change something they don't fully believe in and others are trying to implement it while quietly worrying they're going to lose control of their classroom. Some start to feel like their professional judgment is being replaced by a checklist.

You can feel it in team meetings, where a few people lean in, others go quiet, and the room gets just a little more tense than it used to be. Initiatives start to lose traction. A few classrooms adopt new practices while others remain unchanged and students in one hallway benefit from the improvement while students in the other continue experiencing the same instruction they always have.

Over time, the culture begins to change. Compliance is easy to track, so it quietly becomes the focus. Leaders spend more time managing whether something was done and less time developing the people doing the work.

The emotional cost of this change isn't often discussed openly. Leaders often find themselves spending most of their energy on the same few difficult situations, while the teachers eager to grow receive far less attention. Teachers sense the tension and sometimes respond by lowering expectations as a way of protecting themselves.

Students ultimately feel the impact. When the adults in a system struggle to navigate change together, learning opportunities become uneven from one classroom to the next.

None of this happens because people stopped caring. Leaders and teachers care deeply about their work and the students they serve. The issue is we have long seen resistance as a *problem* to be managed, not as a *clue* as to how we can make it all work.

The Tension Most Leaders Feel

Many leaders experience a tension that seldom gets named out loud.

The work asks you to care about people while also pushing for improvement. You want teachers to feel respected and supported, and at the same time you know students need stronger instruction. Holding those two commitments together can feel harder than anyone prepared you for.

Over time it can start to feel like a choice you have to make: If you lean hard into accountability, relationships can start to strain. If you pull back, initiatives you believe in begin to lose traction. Somewhere in the middle of that tension, you're trying to lead well. You strive to support people without lowering expectations and keep things moving without losing trust. Some days, it feels like you can't quite get it right.

That tension wears people down. Leaders are deeply committed to making a difference. They work hard to build relationships and support teachers in meaningful ways. The issue isn't a lack of compassion or effort.

What many leaders have never been shown is how to hold expectations and humanity at the same time. How to ask people to grow without slipping into compliance-driven leadership. How to stay steady when someone is frustrated, overwhelmed, or pushing back on a change you believe students genuinely need.

This book isn't about moving past resistance by simply being nicer. It isn't about lowering expectations, softening accountability, or sidestepping critical conversations so everyone feels comfortable. And it certainly isn't about becoming someone's therapist in the hope that empathy alone will inspire change.

Too often it feels as though accountability and humanity live on opposite sides of the same line.

This book offers another way.

Who This Book Is For

Some of you reading this book are instructional coaches or teacher leaders who influence change without formal authority. Others are principals, assistant principals, or district leaders who hold positional responsibility for improvement. The dynamics of these roles are different. Coaches often lead through relationships, collaboration, and influence, while administrators carry the authority to set expectations and the responsibility for whether improvement actually happens.

Despite those differences, both roles face the same core challenge: helping educators grow in meaningful ways when compliance alone won't move them forward. Whether you are guiding colleagues through coaching conversations or setting direction for a school or district, the work ultimately requires the same thing. It requires leadership that can support staff through the discomfort they feel when it comes to change.

Throughout the rest of this book, I will use the words leader and coach to refer to anyone responsible for supporting the growth of educators, whether that leadership happens through coaching, collaboration, or positional authority.

As you read, you'll notice I sometimes say *leader*, sometimes *coach*, and other times refer to leadership or coaching moves. I'm not using those words to define a specific role or title. I'm using them more loosely, based on what fits in the moment. In some districts, those roles are clearly defined, and in others they overlap, but the ideas in this book are meant to apply across all of them.

So rather than focusing on whether a section is labeled for a "leader" or a "coach," read for what feels relevant to you and your context.

Leading isn't about heroically showing up as the expert and bestowing knowledge. It's about courageously showing up every day to stand for the potential of each and every one of our educators. It means letting go of how we think things "should" go and asking ourselves a harder question:

What do they need from me to make a real impact?

This book exists to help you answer that question when resistance shows up.

What We've Been Told to Do

Leaders and coaches do not arrive at this point through lack of effort. We arrive here after trying the strategies the profession has taught us to use:

* Strengthen relationships
* Provide better professional development
* Model effective instruction
* Focus energy on the teachers who actively seek support
* Increase accountability

Each of these approaches carries value. In the right circumstances, they can lead to meaningful improvement, yet many leaders eventually notice that these strategies don't always address the deeper issue. A familiar explanation begins to show up: some teachers simply don't want to change. The label "resistant teacher" appears, sometimes spoken aloud and sometimes held privately. That may describe the surface behavior, but it doesn't help leaders decide what to do next.

Over time, working with coaches and leaders across the country, I began to realize something important:

Human beings are wired to grow, but that drive only shows up when the conditions support it. When someone seems unwilling to change, they're protecting something that matters to them.

What looks like resistance is actually a signal.

A Different Way to Understand Resistance

The central belief behind this book is simple:

Resistance is a human experience.

Whenever meaningful change enters a system, people begin asking themselves a series of questions, often without realizing it.

- Does this matter to me?
- Can I succeed at this?
- Do I belong in this work?
- Is growth actually possible here?
- Can I actually change things in this environment?

When those questions remain unanswered, resistance appears. What leaders sometimes interpret as defiance, laziness, or disengagement is often the visible surface of an unmet need.

When I first started coaching, I didn't have that language yet. I just knew something wasn't adding up when I saw resistance.

When resistance showed up, whether I was working with schools in Kentucky or Florida, I started to notice patterns. It showed up when people couldn't see the value of a change, doubted their ability to succeed, felt disconnected from the people around them, lacked a sense of ownership, or struggled to believe growth was possible.

Those patterns eventually became the **Catalyst Mindsets™**.

Rather than treating resistance as behavior that must be managed, this framework invites leaders to interpret resistance as information. A teacher's hesitation or frustration is a clue about a belief that needs support.

Once you begin looking at resistance this way, conversations start to evolve.

What This Book Will Change for You

As you move through this book, resistance will likely begin to feel different.

Situations that once felt confusing start to become clear. Conversations that used to make your shoulders tense may feel easier. You may recognize patterns in how people respond to change and what those reactions might be telling you.

Many leaders I've worked with feel a sense of relief when this change happens. Something finally clicks.

"Oh… that's what's going on."
"This actually makes sense."
"No wonder this hasn't been working."
"This isn't just me."

Resistance starts to feel less personal. You begin to see it as information. What once felt like opposition begins to reveal itself as a signal about what someone may need in order to move forward.

That shift changes the emotional experience of leadership in ways people often notice immediately. The knot in your stomach before a difficult grade-level meeting loosens a little. The dread of walking into certain classrooms starts to fade. Conversations that once spiraled into a standoff begin to feel clearer and more focused on solutions.

Instead of trying to persuade someone or win an argument, you begin listening differently, listening for clues instead of holes. Your attention turns toward what might be underneath the pushback. Curiosity begins to replace frustration, and a steadier presence replaces the reactive energy that so often drives these moments.

Over time the change shows up in the work around you as well. High-stakes conversations tend to become shorter and more productive. Fewer issues circle back week after week. Teachers who once avoided coaching conversations start initiating them. Feedback becomes more honest and less passive, which surprisingly makes it easier to work with.

Gradually the improvement you hoped for begins appearing more consistently across classrooms.

The most meaningful change, though, often happens to you internally.

You learn how to hold high expectations without becoming rigid with people. You develop the ability to stay compassionate while still asking for growth. Critical conversations start to feel less like battles that need to be won and more like moments of understanding that move the work forward.

Many leaders eventually notice a new inner dialogue when they encounter resistance. The thoughts sound something like this:

Okay… don't get defensive.
I don't have to win this.
Just figure out what's going on here.

Once that way of thinking starts to become a habit, resistance stops feeling like something that must be defeated. It becomes something you know how to navigate.

As one leader put it, "I used to think I had to push through resistance. Now I realize I just needed to understand what was underneath it."

Overview of This Book

Part 1: Why Resistance Keeps Showing Up

This section examines why resistance appears so frequently in schools and why it often feels difficult to address in coaching and leadership conversations. It explores how resistance shows up in everyday moments and why we so often misinterpret what we're seeing.

These chapters move the focus from *reacting* to behavior to *understanding* what is driving it, helping leaders move from, "Why isn't this working?" to, "What may be getting in the way?"

Part 2: The Catalyst Mindsets™

This section introduces the five Catalyst Mindsets™ that shape how people respond to change. Each chapter focuses on one mindset and explores how it influences belief and behavior in real situations.

You will learn how to recognize when a mindset is unsupported, what resistance can sound like in coaching conversations, and how to respond in ways that support meaningful progress.

Each chapter is designed to help you see, understand, and act. It begins with the mindset and the belief underneath it, then explores why leaders often struggle to build it, including the Silent Progress Blocker that works against it in schools every day. From there, the chapter moves into application, offering a practical tool, examples in action, coaching guidance, and clear next steps you can use immediately.

> **Bonus Resources**
>
> Additional tools, reflection guides, and coaching supports are available at **thewholeeducator.com/book-resources** to support implementation in day-to-day practice.

As you read, connections to specific teachers, conversations, and moments from your own work will naturally emerge. This book is designed to stay grounded in those real situations. You may choose to move through the book from beginning to end or return to specific sections when a familiar challenge arises. Both approaches support application.

Over time, the framework can enable you to do more than select the right strategy. You can develop a way of seeing resistance: patterns become easier to recognize, conversations become easier to interpret, and moments that once felt unclear begin to make sense.

Once you start seeing resistance through that lens, the work of leading change doesn't feel the same again.

PART 1:
Why Resistance Keeps Showing Up

Chapter 1:
Why Resistance Happens

I Was That Teacher, and I Was Stuck

In my first year teaching, I was resistant. I strutted into my brand-new classroom with big ideas, zero experience, and the unshakable belief that I knew better than everyone around me.

My district required me to teach a specific reading program that I, in my infinite wisdom, didn't feel was best for my students. Professional development? *A waste of time.* Feedback? *For teachers who weren't as naturally gifted as me.* Veteran teachers offering advice? *Cute, but unnecessary.* I was an arrogant twenty-two-year-old straight out of college, and I, frankly, thought I knew best. No one could tell me otherwise.

Then… reality hit. A month into school, my classroom was out of control. My lesson plans crashed daily, and my students were hiding under desks (literally) and ignoring instructions. I was working twelve-hour days to fix the mess I had made. Every day on my way to work, I'd blast my "I believe in you" ballad on repeat while crying into my travel mug of lukewarm coffee.

It was chaotic, and I was exhausted.

I wasn't lazy or apathetic. I was stuck. Stuck in my own assumptions, stuck not trusting the help offered to me, and stuck in the gap between what I thought teaching was going to be and what it actually was. And I wasn't alone.

Teachers all over the nation feel stuck, just like I did. They struggle even when they care deeply and are working hard because something essential is missing.

Some teachers stay in survival mode all school year, keeping their head down and holding it together with duct tape and caffeine. Some are experiencing severe stress and burnout and are one crisis away from losing it. Too many quit the profession altogether, deciding they just weren't "cut out" for teaching. The rare few that break through struggle and resistance have unearthed the mindsets, support, and crystal-clear thinking needed to go from struggling to crushing it.

Unfortunately right now, many schools aren't helping teachers break through. They're trying to "compliance" their way out of resistance. Consequently, nothing is changing. The cost of staying in this cycle is serious. Leaders feel frustrated at repeated failures. Teachers are disempowered and disillusioned and are leaving the profession on a daily basis. Most importantly, students are not learning enough in class.

It doesn't have to be this way.

The solution starts in how the adults in our districts and schools interact with each other. I know you're already trying your best to meet the many needs of your teachers, and in some cases it doesn't seem to make a difference. It takes effort to keep your cool with the teacher who insists, "My kids can't do it" or who responds to new teaching strategies with, "I've tried this before, and it didn't work." You walk away from these dissatisfying and draining conversations wanting to shove cookies in your face and watch true crime. You didn't sign up to be a resistance manager, but here you are.

Most leaders don't fully understand resistance, so they end up chasing symptoms instead of addressing what's actually underneath it.

The Mistake We Keep Making: Thinking Resistance Is Bad

First of all, I want to normalize resistance. It is a natural and predictable part of being human. We all (yes, even you) experience resistance throughout our lives. Think about the appointment you keep meaning to schedule but haven't. The message you've reread three times but still haven't responded to. The task you know matters, but somehow keeps getting pushed to tomorrow. So don't ask *if* you experience resistance. Ask *when*.

Looking back at my first year teaching, my resistance didn't feel irrational. It felt responsible because I genuinely believed I was doing what was best for my students.

Another reason resistance is perfectly natural in our teachers is because of who we hire. Think about the types of teachers you want to hire at your school. You want them to be adaptable and flexible, and also analytical and strategic. All these qualities require critical thinking, and we want to hire teachers who thoughtfully evaluate situations. However, when a decision comes down the pipeline that *they didn't choose*, we get upset when they don't immediately adopt it. We get frustrated with the pushback and slow (or nonexistent) implementation and often label the teacher resistant when, in fact, they're often simply grappling with the change. They're grappling with whether it's worth the risk to do it, whether they have the necessary skills, or even simply understanding why the change is happening.

We forget that we want our beautiful critical thinkers to think!

The main message I want you to get before diving into the world of understanding resistance is this: **Resistance. Isn't. Bad.**

Let's put aside the "badness" and "wrongness" we have about resistance and do the work to understand the humanity of the teachers we work with. When change happens, resistance shows up for one reason:

Unmet needs.

You experience resistance. I experience resistance. In education, we have demonized pushback and resistance and elevated direction-following and compliance. When we do this, we step over the very humanity of our teachers, immediately reducing trust, diminishing relationships, and going against the heart of education.

Because education is fundamentally a human experience.

A note about my language:

I use the phrase *teachers experiencing resistance* instead of simply *resistant teachers*. I don't call people resistant. Labels stick in unhelpful ways. Resistance isn't who someone is. It's an experience someone is having. That experience can change at any moment if we know how to support someone through that.

When you are experiencing a lot of resistance to change, you're not missing the perfect protocol or coaching tool. You're missing humanity. You're missing the very human connection that is the foundation underneath everything we do. When someone experiences resistance, we tend to move away and disconnect. We call that being "professional." We keep our distance and "kill them with kindness." Instead, we must move toward those experiencing resistance. We must reach out and connect. That's the only authentic way to reduce resistance and empower our educators.

Building Buy-In Isn't Enough

For years, we've treated buy-in as the goal. If teachers agree, we assume the work will stick. Yet agreement isn't the same as ownership, and agreement alone doesn't sustain change.

I can think of moments in my early teaching where I agreed with what I was being asked to do. I could nod along in a meeting, see the logic, even say, "Yeah, that makes sense." But I hadn't taken ownership of it. Once I closed my classroom door, I went right back to what felt familiar. The change made perfect sense to the person leading it. It just didn't feel like mine yet.

Ownership doesn't appear overnight. It develops along a continuum, called the Levels of Engagement, created by Dr. Chris Jones.

Educators operate at different levels of engagement, influenced by factors like voice, choice, agency, and their underlying beliefs about the work. Understanding these levels can help leaders diagnose where people are and what kind of support will move them forward.

Levels of Engagement

Adapted from Dr. Chris Jones' Levels of Engagement.

1. **Sabotage**: At this level, educators actively work against the change or quietly undermine it.
2. **Defiance**: Here, teachers resist implementation more passively. They may close their doors, revert to old practices, or comply on paper while doing something entirely different in reality.
3. **Compliance**: Teachers follow directions, attend required trainings, and complete tasks, but without emotional or intellectual investment. You can hear them say, "Just tell me what to do."
4. **Buy-In**: This is where most traditional leadership stops. Buy-in happens when a leader chooses the direction and successfully convinces teachers to *want* to implement it. Teachers are implementing someone else's decision they happen to agree with.

These first four levels of engagement (Sabotage, Defiance, Compliance, and Buy-In) sit on the lower half of the continuum. What they have in common is a lack of real voice and choice in the change. Change is still externally driven, and teachers are reacting to it rather than co-creating it.

The difference between Buy-In and Ownership comes down to agency. The line between them marks a critical point: below it, leaders hold the power; above it, teachers begin to share it. From this point forward, educators move from being managed participants to empowered contributors.

5. **Ownership**: Teachers take personal responsibility for outcomes. They bring ideas, take initiative, and adapt the work to fit their students' needs. Leadership still provides direction, but teachers shape how the work happens.
6. **Commitment**: Teachers are deeply invested in the success of the change because they see themselves as coauthors of it. They

seek feedback, take risks, and hold themselves to high standards. The work is no longer about compliance. It's about contribution.

7. **Leadership**: At this highest level, educators model ownership for others. They mentor peers, influence school culture, and sustain momentum. Their engagement is contagious and inspires others to move up the continuum.

When we can name where people are, we can actually see progress. Moving from defiance to compliance is progress, but the goal isn't to stop there. This work is about building ownership.

Why Resistance Feels Impossible to Crack

There are three reasons leaders struggle to break through resistance:

1. We misunderstand it.

As I shared earlier, resistance isn't the enemy. It's simply about having unmet needs and teachers' earnest attempts to feel safe and meet those needs.

2. We misapply strategies.

If a teacher experiences resistance when trying a new engagement strategy because they're worried about losing control of the class, but you interpret it as them being difficult... *again*... then your solution might involve heavy accountability. The solution in no way meets the teacher's needs.

3. We don't slow down enough to diagnose the real issue.

We're all so darn busy, we haven't stopped long enough to look at what's actually going on. All of the coaches and leaders I've ever worked with are clearly intelligent, driven people. So why do we keep doing the same things, expecting something different? I know what it's like to feel the pressure to get results and feeling like there's not enough resources, time, or sanity to get it all done. So what do we do? We run around, trying our best to get people on board with some semblance of good teaching. We worry that if we slow down, we won't get everything done. This behavior is the very reason we don't achieve the results we want.

Your brain on resistance

Do you remember those old ads with the egg in a frying pan and the headline, "This is your brain on drugs?" Well, this is your brain on resistance. Or, more accurately, this is *our* brain on resistance. When we experience resistance, the brain responds automatically. Parts of the brain that focus on protection and survival become more active, while the parts responsible for reflection, logic, problem solving, and flexibility go quieter. This happens fast and without us choosing it.

This means what looks like pushback, avoidance, or shutdown is often the brain trying to keep us safe. It's protecting us. Here's why that matters: when someone is in that protective state, we can explain, justify, or coach all we want, but it won't land the way we hope it will. We're trying to engage a part of the brain that doesn't speak logic. Its one job is to keep us safe.

This is why "connection before correction" is so important. It taps into how people are wired to respond. Before someone can take in feedback, consider a new idea, or try something different, their brain has to feel safe enough to do so. If we skip that step, we're not coaching. We're talking to a brain that's busy trying to protect itself.

The Three-Step Process for Navigating Resistance

This book can help you understand why resistance happens and what to do about it. Instead of pushing against resistance, you can learn how to move through it. As we discussed earlier, the goal of our schools isn't blind compliance. This work is about helping people show up, think, and engage in the work in a real way. You can learn how to diagnose what's actually happening and, with compassion and nonjudgment, respond in a way that gets to the root issue.

This work isn't for the faint of heart.

At its core, this process comes down to three steps:

- First, notice and address your own reaction to the situation.
- Then, diagnose what's underneath their resistance.
- Finally, respond in a way that meets that need.

Before you can respond to resistance well, you have to know what kind of resistance you're looking at. In the next chapter, we'll get underneath the surface and explore the core forms resistance takes, so you're not guessing anymore.

Chapter 2:
The Roots of Resistance

Why One-Size-Fits-All Doesn't Work

As we begin to understand why resistance happens, we have to start at the root.

One of the biggest mistakes I see schools make is relying on one-size-fits-all strategies to address resistance. We already know that approach falls short with students, yet it shows up all the time in how we work with adults.

The reality is that resistance doesn't come from one place. When we treat it like it does, we end up circling the same problems, trying strategy after strategy without getting anywhere different.

The real work is underneath the behavior. What you see first is push-back, hesitation, or avoidance. Beneath that, something else is happening. There's uncertainty. There are mental calculations about what feels risky, what feels worth it, and whether they can actually do what's being asked.

When we stay at the surface, resistance has a way of returning, sometimes louder than before. When we slow down long enough to understand what's driving it, we start to see a different path forward.

We're going to spend the time either way.

We can spend it reacting to the same problems, or we can spend it understanding what's really driving them.

Skill Is Not the Same as Will

In the previous chapter, we landed on this: resistance is caused by un-met needs. The natural next question is: Which need is going unmet?

When a teacher is stuck and progress slows, here is the first question I ask leaders: *Is this a gap in skill, or a gap in will?*

This book focuses primarily on will. The willingness to try, to change, and do the work when it gets uncomfortable.

Here's why that distinction matters.

Schools are built to grow skill, and most leaders and coaches already know how to do this well. If a teacher needs support with engagement strategies, you model. If differentiation is a struggle, you sit down to-gether and plan it out. If teaching practice needs refining, you practice side by side. There are clear, familiar ways to help someone get better at the craft.

Resistance shows up differently.

On the surface, it often reads like a skill issue. A lesson falls flat, a strategy never quite makes it into practice, a commitment sounds solid in the meeting and then fades once the classroom door closes. It's easy to assume the person just doesn't know how.

Look a little closer, and a different story usually starts to emerge.

Something else is usually at play. You can see it in the hesitation before trying something new, or in the quiet uncertainty about how it will go. Sometimes there's a quiet calculation happening in the background: *Is this worth it? What happens if it doesn't work? Can I actually pull this off with my students?*

A teacher can know exactly what to do and still not do it. In those moments, we often add more modeling, more planning, more practice. What's showing up is useful information about what's going on beneath the surface.

When you pay attention to it, that information usually points to an unmet need.

This is where many of us get stuck. We reach for strategies designed to build skill, hoping they'll move things forward, and instead we find ourselves having the same conversations again and again. Nothing really improves, and it starts to feel like pushing a boulder that won't budge, which can feel equal parts frustrating and exhausting.

Part of the problem is that there isn't much guidance for the people in the middle of it. Coaches and administrators are trying to lead change while carrying the emotional weight that comes with it. Many are walking out of conversations thinking, *I know something deeper is going on here, but I just can't name it.*

There are plenty of resources on *what* and *how* to teach. There are far fewer on how to navigate the human side of change when willingness is low.

The cost of that gap is real. We can't keep cycling teachers out of the profession in a time when schools are already facing significant shortages. When resistance is misunderstood, we lose more than momentum. We lose people.

There is a real need for this work in education.

That's the work of this book.

The Five Forms of Resistance

You try something that worked with one teacher, and it falls flat with another. You adjust, try again, and still feel like you're missing something. After a while, it can start to feel unpredictable, but it isn't. Part of what makes navigating resistance so frustrating is that feeling of not quite being able to pin down what's actually going on.

Underneath the surface, resistance tends to follow patterns. Once you start to see those patterns, things change. What used to feel confusing starts to feel more readable. You stop reacting in the moment and start paying attention to what the behavior might be pointing to.

Here are the five most common forms I see.

Irrelevance

This is what it looks like when the change doesn't feel meaningful.

There's no clear connection to what matters in their classroom or with their students, so the work is perceived as a demand rather than something worth investing in. Even strong teachers can disengage here, not out of defiance but out of disconnection from purpose.

You'll hear irrelevance in the questions:

- "What's the point?"
- "How does this actually help my kids?"
- "Is this really worth the time?"

Disconnection

This is what it looks like when people don't feel a sense of connection to the people around them.

There's a lack of trust, support, or shared understanding, so the work feels isolating rather than collaborative. Even strong teachers can pull back here, not out of defiance but because they don't feel seen, supported, or part of something with others.

Sometimes it shows up quietly, with short answers, polite agreement, and a general lack of real engagement.

Sometimes you'll hear disconnection in the questions:

- "Why am I the only one being asked to do this?"
- "Does anyone actually understand what my classroom is like?"
- "Who is this really for?"
- "It won't matter what I say anyway."

Doubt

Here, the question is whether it will actually work.

There's a belief, sometimes spoken and sometimes not, that the effort won't lead to the outcome being promised. That belief shapes everything that follows. If success doesn't feel possible, trying starts to feel pointless.

You'll hear it in statements like these:

- "I've tried that before. It didn't work."
- "The kids can't do it."
- "That sounds great in theory, but we don't have what we need."

Comfort Zone

This form is less about the result and more about the experience of getting there.

This is what it looks like when the change pushes someone beyond what feels familiar or manageable. The work may feel uncertain, overwhelming, or risky, so staying with what's known feels safer than trying something new. Even strong teachers can get stuck here because stepping outside their comfort zone feels like too big of a leap.

You'll hear comfort zone in the questions:

- "What if this doesn't work?"
- "Can I just stick with what I know works?"
- "This feels like a lot right now."
- "I hate not knowing what I'm doing."

Helplessness

This is what it looks like when people stop believing their actions will make a difference. Whether that belief is grounded in reality or shaped by past experiences, the work begins to feel out of their hands, and effort and initiative start to fade. At times, this grows from a genuine lack of support. Other times, it comes from something less obvious, like overload. When everything feels urgent, options multiply, and expectations pile up, people can shut down. What feels like a lack of resources is often people hitting their limit.

You'll hear helplessness in the statements:

- "There's nothing I can do."
- "Nothing ever changes around here."

Before we move on...

These forms aren't meant as labels to assign to people. They're patterns you start to recognize over time. At least, that's how it's been for me. What used to feel like one big category of resistance started to break into something more specific, more readable.

I've misread every single one of these. I've assumed it was a skill issue and jumped straight to solutions, only to realize later I was solving the wrong problem. The work is staying with it long enough to understand what you're actually seeing.

What the Forms of Resistance Reveal

Over the years, I've seen a pattern in professional development, and if I'm being honest, I've been part of the pattern, too. We give coaches and leaders a set of resistance strategies and expect those strategies to work across the board. It makes sense. Someone is resisting, so we reach for a move that's supposed to help them move forward.

Sometimes it does. Something changes in the moment, the conversation feels productive, and you walk away thinking, *Okay, that worked.*

But then it shows up again, sometimes in a slightly different way and often a little stronger, and that's usually when things start to feel off, like we're doing the right things but not quite getting where we want to go. It starts to feel like we were working *around* resistance instead of actually *understanding* it.

This is where the Forms of Resistance begin to matter.

Naming the form gives us language for what we're seeing. It helps us move out of that vague sense that "something's off" and into something more specific. But Forms only tell us what resistance *looks like*. They don't tell us what's *driving* it.

This is where it can still fall apart.

You can correctly name the Form of Resistance and still feel stuck on what to do next. You can respond to the behavior in front of you and still find yourself having the same conversation again a week later because the form isn't the root.

Underneath every form is something deeper. There's a set of beliefs about what feels risky, what feels worth it, and what feels possible. These beliefs are what we mean by mindsets. Each Form of Resistance is driven by an unsupported mindset. Once you start to see that, the whole picture becomes clearer.

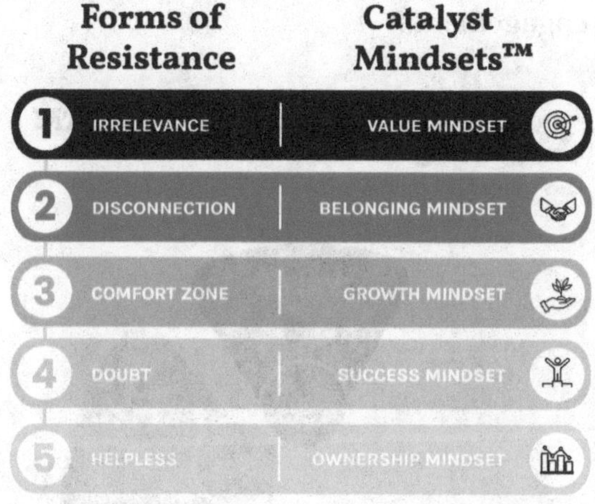

The question moves from *"What should I do here?"* to *"What belief might be driving this?"*

It's worth slowing down for a second here because the word *mindset* gets used in a lot of different ways.

A mindset isn't effort, resilience, a set of strategies, or even a collection of habits. Those things are influenced by mindsets, but they aren't the mindset itself. At its core, a mindset is a belief.

That belief lives somewhere very real in the brain. Patterns of thinking get reinforced over time. Scientists commonly use the phrase, "What wires together, fires together" to describe how neural pathways strengthen with repeated use. It's a simple way of pointing to something important. The more a belief is practiced, the more automatic it becomes. Understanding the science helps, but what you do next is what really matters.

If we want to see different behavior, we have to understand the belief driving it.

This book focuses on the five beliefs underlying resistance. I call them the Catalyst Mindsets™ because they move people out of resistance and back into engagement.

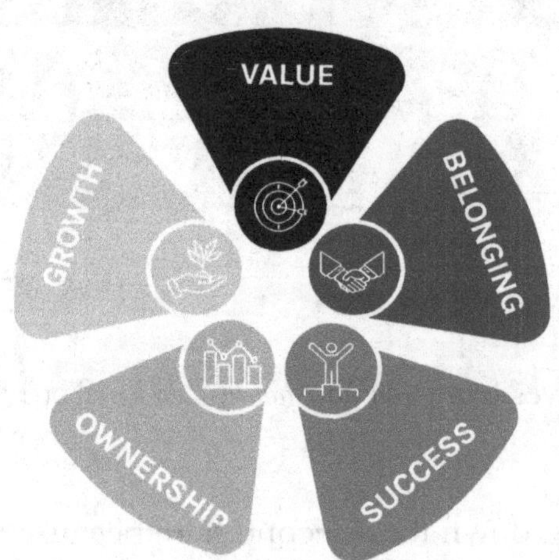

- **Value Mindset**: I believe this has value for me.
- **Belonging Mindset**: I believe I belong here.
- **Success Mindset**: I believe I can be successful.

- **Growth Mindset**: I believe I can improve.
- **Ownership Mindset**: I believe I can change things by taking responsibility.

You can see how this plays out in everyday life, not just in schools.

Take something as simple as people-pleasing. If the underlying belief is, *If I say no, I'll disappoint people and risk being left out,* that belief doesn't stay in the background. It starts shaping how everything gets interpreted. *They'll think I'm difficult. It's easier to just say yes. I don't want to rock the boat.*

Those thoughts lead somewhere. You overcommit, agree to things you don't actually want to do, and show up with a smile and leave feeling drained. When you shift the belief, even slightly, everything downstream starts to shift with it. The thoughts, decisions, and experiences change.

Real change happens at that level.

When I'm trying to understand what's going on for someone, I listen closely to what they say. But I've learned to pay more attention to what they do, especially when the two don't quite line up, because that's usually where the belief is showing itself most clearly.

If I have to choose where to look, I start with behavior. That's where beliefs tend to leave their fingerprints.

Stop spinning your wheels. Let's get to the root. The next step is learning how to identify what's actually driving the resistance so you can solve the right problem. There's no point in applying strategies if you don't know which mindset is underneath it.

Resistance is part of the process. Mishandling it is what creates the real problems.

At this point, it can start to feel like a lot to hold, with five forms, five beliefs, and five different ways resistance shows up. To make this easier to use in real time, I've created a simple one-page quick reference that connects each form of resistance to the mindset underneath it and the tool that supports it.

You can find the Catalyst Mindsets™ Quick Reference Chart at thewholeeducator.com/book-resources.

Chapter 3: How We Get in the Way

Now let's turn our focus for a moment. We've spent time looking at resistance and where it comes from. Before we go any further, there's another layer we need to look at, and it's a little closer to home.

This next part will require a level of honesty we don't always slow down to practice. At some point, we have to be willing to look at ourselves in the middle of all of this.

Even with the best intentions, we can make this harder than it needs to be.

As coaches and leaders, we are deeply invested in supporting our educators. It's why we chose this work. Still, in the middle of real conversations, especially when resistance shows up, something else tends to slip in almost automatically. It's quick, almost unnoticeable at first, but once you see it, you can't really unsee it.

The shoulds.

You can probably hear them already:

He should know better.
They should already be doing this.
She should want to grow.

They don't usually come in as a full thought. It's more like a subtle change in your body, a tightening, a gnawing feeling that something isn't lining up the way you think it's supposed to. To be fair, the expectations themselves aren't the issue. The work and the outcomes matter, and there's a real urgency to getting this right.

When those *shoulds* take over, curiosity starts to fade, often without us noticing. Instead of wondering what might be getting in the way, we move quickly into deciding what should already be happening. It's a small change, but it changes how we listen, how we respond, and what we're even able to see. Once that lens is in place, it becomes much harder to understand what's actually going on beneath the surface.

The difference between supporting someone and "shoulding" them can feel subtle, but they lead to completely different outcomes.

Support = Expectation + Curiosity

We have an expectation and there's a clear picture of what we're aiming for. We get curious about how we can support this person and try to understand what might be getting in the way. It sounds like this:

I wonder what this person needs to be successful.

Shoulds = Expectation + Judgment

The expectation is still here, too, which is part of why this can be so easy to miss. It feels like we're doing the same thing, but something important starts to feel different. Instead of asking curious questions, we start evaluating. We decide whether what's happening is good or bad, right or wrong, or acceptable or not. This judgment begins to shape everything that follows.

This is the part I had to learn and, honestly, relearn.

Shoulds don't just stay in your head as thoughts. They show up in your tone, your questions, and the way you interpret what someone says. They quietly narrow your view, often without you realizing it. Before long, you're responding to your interpretation instead of what's actually happening, which is where things start to get tricky.

Shoulds are, in their own way, a form of resistance. When we respond from "the shoulds", we tend to stay stuck. We react to what we can see instead of getting curious about what's underneath. And the more we push, the more resistance we get back.

At some point, I had to pause and admit that I was contributing to the very dynamic I was trying to change. That realization wasn't comfortable, but it changed how I approached everything after that. If we want something different to happen, it has to start here with us.

This work isn't about lowering expectations. It shifts our attention to how those expectations are actually being held.

This is where the Expectation Continuum becomes useful. It gives you a way to notice where you are in the moment and make a different choice, to move back toward curiosity without losing sight of what matters.

The work is coming back to where they are right now, even when that's not where we hoped they'd be.

You can't coach who you wish they were.

The Resistance Map

If we want to coach well, we have to go first. This is easy to say and often harder to actually do.

Looking at someone else's resistance is much easier. You can name it, analyze it, feel pretty confident you've got a read on what's going on. I've done this more times than I can count. Turning that same lens on yourself feels different: a little less clear and a little more uncomfortable. There's more at stake when it's you, and that's usually the moment I know I need to pay attention.

Every coaching move you make is shaped by what's happening inside you at that moment. The questions you ask, the tone you use, even the decision to lean in or pull back all come from somewhere. When your own resistance is active, it has a way of showing up, whether you intend it to or not, which is why we start here.

This is what the Resistance Map is for.

It's a simple way to notice what's happening in you when coaching or leadership gets hard, so you can respond with more intentionality instead of reacting on autopilot. There's a simple truth underneath all of this: *you can't shift what you can't see.*

Resistance doesn't just live in the people we support. It starts with us more often than we realize.

Step 1: Notice Where It Shows Up

Start by thinking about moments in your coaching or leadership work that tend to feel harder than others. The moments where something feels tense or frustrating, where you hesitate or you feel yourself pushing, pulling back, or second-guessing.

As you read the situations below, pay attention to your reactions without overthinking it. This isn't a test; it's more of a gut check:

Where do you feel tension?
Where do you hesitate or avoid?
Where do you push harder, try to control, or start to shut down?

Here are some common places resistance shows up in coaching work:

- Delivering hard feedback and holding accountability
- Navigating resistance or skepticism
- Taking risks and modeling imperfect practice
- Letting go of control and trusting teacher autonomy
- Managing overwhelm, time, and emotional load
- Receiving feedback about your own coaching

Step 2: Name the Pattern

Now, take one of those moments and get a little more specific.

Ask yourself: *What's actually happening within me at this moment?*

When you sit with that question, you'll start to notice patterns. Most of the time, what shows up connects back to one or more of the five Forms of Resistance:

- **Irrelevance** – This doesn't feel worth the effort.
- **Disconnection** – This feels risky to the relationship.
- **Doubt** – I'm not sure I can be successful.
- **Comfort Zone** – I'm afraid of unknown reactions and the messy process.
- **Helplessness** – I don't see what would actually change.

You might see more than one, which is completely normal.

Step 3: Look Closer

If it helps, you can walk through a few specific coaching moments:

- **Delivering hard feedback**

  When a difficult conversation is needed, what shows up first?

  Where do you lean in, and where do you pull back?

- **Navigating pushback**

  When someone questions the work, what comes up?

  Do you get more forceful, more cautious, or something else?

- **Taking risks**

  When there's a chance of getting it wrong publicly, what happens?

  Do you move toward it or away from it?

- **Letting go of control**

  When someone tries it their way, what reactions show up?

  What makes it hard to step back?

- **Managing overwhelm**

  When everything feels like too much, what's your first move?

  Where do you feel stuck?

- **Receiving feedback**

  When someone gives you feedback on your coaching, what happens immediately after you hear it?

You don't need to answer all of the questions. The goal at this point is to start to notice patterns.

Step 4: Reflect on What You're Seeing

Now zoom out for a moment.

Across these situations, what stands out?

- Which form of resistance shows up most often?

- Where do you feel the strongest reaction?
- What surprised you?
- Which moments feel the most unpleasant or most draining?

There's nothing wrong with any of this. Resistance showing up for you is part of being human. You're gathering useful information that will shape how you show up with your educators.

A quick reminder…

This doesn't just apply to coaching. Once you start seeing these patterns, you'll notice them everywhere.

- In conversations with colleagues
- At home
- In how you respond to feedback
- In how you handle stress, time, and expectations

Part of what makes this work so powerful is that it travels with you.

Where This Leads

At the root of all of this is something simple, even if it doesn't always feel that way in the moment.

Resistance is driven by unmet needs.

Which means the work doesn't start with fixing someone else. It starts a little closer to home. This is usually the part where we want to move too quickly to fix it, to figure it out, to do something with what we just noticed. But when we skip past this part, we miss what's actually going on.

There's something about staying here a little longer, letting yourself really see the pattern before trying to change it. These reactions are pointing to something underneath. Once you start to see that more clearly, you start to respond differently. You're not just reacting to what's happening in front of you anymore. You're starting to understand what's driving it.

Reflection Questions

1. What are your honest "shoulds" about your educators, your colleagues, and yourself?
2. Pick one person. Ask yourself, *What might they need to be successful here?*

This work keeps expectations high while asking for an honest look at what's getting in the way, so you can identify the unmet need underneath it and shift the behavior at its source.

PART 2:
The Catalyst Mindsets™

Chapter 4:
Value Mindset

It Was Never About the Smartboard

On the first day at my new school, I walked into my classroom, turned to my principal, and said, "Whatever you do, don't give me a classroom with a Smartboard."

Every classroom had one.

I had just returned to the United States after three years of teaching overseas in South America and Africa. While I was gone, what I called the "Smart Revolution" had happened. Smartboards. Smartphones. Apps for everything. I came back with my metallic blue flip phone and a death grip on it. No one was going to dupe me into looking like I was talking into a calculator. Absolutely not.

In the schools where I had been teaching abroad, electricity was optional on a daily basis. My students learned from textbooks, notebook paper, and each other, and they learned well. So when I stepped back into a system that seemed obsessed with screens, something in me tensed.

I wouldn't use the Smartboard for an entire year.

It felt like each weekly staff meeting introduced a new app. I'd sit there quietly, watching my colleagues get excited about "engagement tools," rolling my eyes just enough to feel morally superior, biding my time until I could return to my classroom and change nothing. My little technology rebellion felt justified.

Looking back now, it seems small. But at the time, it felt enormous.

I was resisting a tool and protecting my identity. What mattered to me was knowing I was a good teacher and that my students were learning. The Smartboard felt like a threat to that. It felt risky, and at that point, nothing about it felt worth that risk.

I had built a reputation as a competent, capable educator in environments that demanded creativity without technology. If kids learned beautifully from me overseas, why did I suddenly need a shiny gadget to prove I could teach? Somewhere in the back of my mind was this fear: *If I embrace this, do I lose the part of me that knows how to teach without it?*

My resistance centered on control, competence, and holding on to what had made me good. The Smartboard didn't feel relevant to what I already found important. It didn't feel worth the cost of reworking everything I knew.

This change lacked value for me.

What helped me engage was a conversation. My assistant principal, someone I deeply respected, sat in my classroom one afternoon and simply talked with me. She didn't diminish me or imply I was behind. She saw my commitment, respected my experience, and honored the teacher I already was.

In that space, I relaxed.

The future my students were walking into had changed. Preparing them well might require me to change, too. Once my identity felt safe, I could let go.

That's when I finally gave the Smartboard a shot.

The Mindset: Value

Value shows up when the work feels connected to what matters.

When what's being asked aligns with what matters to them, the effort feels worthwhile. When it doesn't, the same effort feels imposed. The belief underneath the Value Mindset is simple:

I believe this has value for me.

Think about it this way. I find value in physical exercise because it gives me energy and helps me feel strong. The action connects to something I care about. I don't find value in knitting a scarf because I'd rather spend that time doing other things and could easily just buy one instead. It simply doesn't feel worth it to me.

Research shows people tend to experience value through a few common lenses:

- This is useful.
- This is personally important.
- This is interesting.
- This is connected to something bigger.
- This won't cost me too much.

When none of those are present, even good work can feel like a burden.

In schools, an unmet need for value shows up quickly. If a teacher cannot connect an initiative to one of these lenses, it will feel like one more thing added to their plate. Leaders create value by helping educators connect the work to what they already care about.

The goal is helping people make meaning of the work, not just getting better compliance. Value sticks when people can see it for themselves and internalize it.

Why Leaders Struggle to Support This Mindset

Most of us were trained to focus on implementation. When a change is introduced, we most often clarify the plan, explain the research, and reinforce the expectation. When questions come up, the instinct is to explain the strategy more clearly.

Two things tend to get in the way of building value.

First, we project our own priorities onto others. If something matters to us, we assume it *should* matter to them, too. Second, we assume that if the benefits of a change are obvious to us, they *should* be obvious to everyone else.

Unfortunately, value doesn't work that way.

Just because something makes sense to us doesn't mean it feels meaningful to others. When leaders assume the logic of the change should be enough, we unintentionally skip the step that actually builds value: helping educators connect the work to what matters to them.

The Silent Progress Blocker: Compliance Culture

A leader makes a thoughtful decision. The reasoning is solid, the research makes sense, and the goal is clear. Maybe the district has invested heavily in a new curriculum or launched an initiative to strengthen student learning.

Then the rollout begins. Expectations are communicated, timelines are set, and accountability structures are put in place. I often hear leaders say things such as, "People take ownership when they're held accountable," or "If we explain the decision clearly, teachers should get on board."

Those statements sound reasonable, but beneath them is a belief from which many systems operate: accountability alone creates ownership.

What usually follows is familiar. Teachers comply, but they don't commit. They complete the task, but the work never fully becomes theirs. The conversation moves to logistics and requirements. You hear, "Is this required?" and "Just tell me what to do," instead of deeper questions such as, "How will this help my students?" or "How can I make this my own?"

This is compliance culture.

Explaining harder doesn't make people care. Compliance systems ask people to act before they have had the chance to decide whether the work matters to them. When leaders assume that clear logic creates commitment, they skip the step that builds value: helping educators connect the work to what matters to them.

When value has not formed, accountability begins to feel like pressure and loses its sense of shared responsibility. Even when educators care deeply, the connection to what matters to them hasn't been made. You can require action, but you cannot require meaning. When meaning is missing, resistance follows.

It doesn't matter what you say, if what you say doesn't matter *to them*.

The Cost of Getting This Wrong

There is a great cost to leaving the Value Mindset unsupported. The work becomes compliance-driven instead of purpose-driven. We start spending more time reminding than supporting, and extrinsic motivators replace meaning. Incentives, pressure, and monitoring begin driving behavior, and purpose starts to fade. We feel like we're constantly pushing momentum uphill.

We start to see commitment become situational, people engaging only when they are closely monitored. Teachers follow directions, but the work is hardly ever adapted for their students. Implementation is shallow and short-lived, and teachers ask compliance questions instead of the impact questions we want them to ask. Instead of "Will this help students?" they ask:

- "Is this required?"
- "Is this being evaluated?"
- "How long do we have to do this?"

Resistance shows up as delayed follow-through, surface-level effort, and quiet disengagement behind closed doors. Teachers begin picking and choosing what to implement based on what feels relevant to *them*, disengaging from anything that feels disconnected from *their* priorities. Inevitably, our priorities as leaders get left behind.

As a result, alignment begins to fracture. "This is just the new thing" becomes the default narrative. Cynicism spreads faster than momentum. Initiative fatigue accelerates because nothing feels worth the effort. Pushback sounds like exhaustion: "This is just one more thing."

Underneath all of this is something we rarely say out loud.

It is frustrating to work with educators who do not see the value in changes that could significantly impact student learning. You can clearly see the importance of the change, and every day it does not happen, students miss opportunities.

So you try more:

- More professional development
- More coaching
- More modeling
- More explaining

Nothing changes.

Staying in that cycle costs time, energy, and momentum. It drains us because we care deeply about students. It is just as frustrating for the educator whose needs are not being met.

Over time, culture drifts from purpose-driven to expectation-driven. Coaching conversations revolve around task compliance instead of growth. Professional learning begins to feel like something *done to* teachers instead of something we *built with* them.

And everyone ends up tired.

The Shift

So how do we start to build a sense of value for our staff when implementing change?

Stop pushing compliance, isolated accountability, and "because we have to." When value is missing, effort becomes minimal, initiative drops, and conversations start to sound like, "Just tell me what you want."

Start helping educators reconnect the work to what they already care about and navigate what would make the change worth it. Value is created through alignment, not persuasion. When educators see how a change supports what matters to them (their students, identity, sense of competence, or time) they engage. They adapt and persist when it gets hard.

This change takes hold through understanding, as educators begin to see the connection between the work and what already matters to them.

The Core Idea

Find what matters to them.

The Practice

The Resistance Signal

In real time, this form of resistance has a recognizable sound. You might hear teachers say:

- "I don't really see how this helps my students."
- "We've got bigger problems than this."
- "This is just another initiative that will disappear next year."
- "I'm not against it, I just don't see the point."
- "This isn't worth the time it's going to take."

When you hear language like this, it is important to pause rather than react.

The instinct in these moments is often to move quickly into "fixing" with a strategy, defending the research, or reinforcing the urgency of the initiative. Most of us have been trained to do exactly that. This is usually a value problem.

The coaching cue is simple, but not always easy: slow down and understand what matters to them. Before offering ideas or solutions, consider what they might be protecting, what feels at risk, and what would make this work feel worthwhile from their perspective. Moving straight to persuasion reinforces compliance culture. Staying in curiosity helps you hear what actually matters to them.

The Tool: The Value Triangle

Before you move to strategy, take a step back and get specific about what creates value from their perspective. This is where the **Value Triangle** comes in. It gives you a way to surface what's already driving their thinking and identify what will make the work feel relevant, meaningful, and worth the effort.

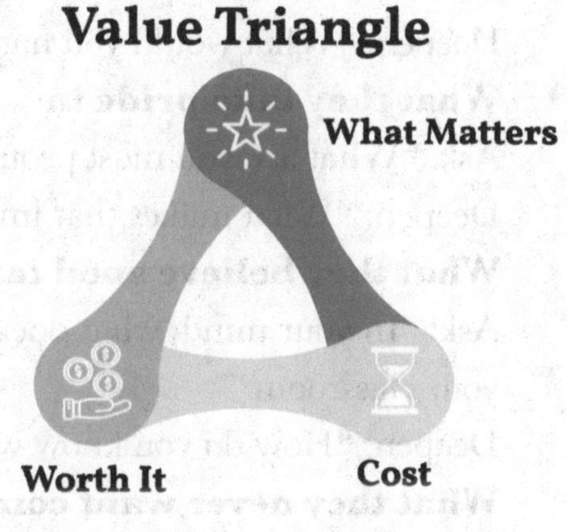

What Matters to Them

You're listening for what they care about, what they feel responsible for, what they take pride in, what they believe good teaching looks like, or what they never want compromised. This is about honoring their professional center of gravity. You're not diagnosing the problem yet. Here are questions you can ask to uncover what matters most:

First decide what you're listening for, then ask a question that helps surface it.

- **What they care about**

  Ask: "What do you care most about in this situation?"

  Deepen: "When you picture it going really well, what's happening for students?"

- **What they feel responsible for**

  Ask: "What are you feeling responsible for here?"

  Deepen: "What do you feel you have to get right, no matter what?"

- **What they want to hold onto**

  Ask: "What feels important to hold onto as things shift?"

  Deepen: "What would you hate to see get diluted or lost?"

- **What they take pride in**

  Ask: "What are you most proud of in your teaching?"

  Deepen: "What makes that important to you?"

- **What they believe good teaching looks like**

  Ask: "In your mind, what does strong instruction look like in your classroom?"

  Deepen: "How do you know when you're doing it well?"

- **What they never want compromised**

  Ask: "What feels nonnegotiable for you?"

  Deepen: "Why is that so important to you?"

Stay curious, and don't rush past this. Don't move to strategy, defend the initiative, or correct their thinking. If you miss what matters to them, very little else you do will make a difference. Let them fully articulate what they care about.

What It Might Cost

You're listening for what feels risky, exposed, or vulnerable. This is about naming what they're afraid they could lose.

First decide what kind of cost you're hearing, then ask a question that helps surface it. Some common costs are: time, energy, control, confidence, relationships, and results.

- **Time pressure or overload**
  Ask: "Where does this fit into everything else on your plate right now?"
  Deepen: "What would you have to move, drop, or stretch to make space for this?"
  When someone says, "I don't have time," don't argue about the calendar. Get curious about their priorities.
- **Energy depletion or burnout**
  Ask: "How much capacity do you feel like you have for something new right now?"
  Deepen: "What would need to change for this not to feel draining?"
- **Loss of control or stability**
  Ask: "What feels uncertain about this shift?"
  Deepen: "What part of this feels hardest to let go of?"
- **Emotional or relational strain**
  Ask: "What feels stressful about this right now?"
  Deepen: "What feels like it's on the line for you?"
- **Fear of failure or feeling incompetent**
  Ask: "What worries you about trying this?"
  Deepen: "What would feel most uncomfortable if it didn't go well?"

Stay focused and don't minimize the risk. When the cost is named, it starts to lose power.

What Would Make It Worth It

You're listening for what would create personal payoff.

Start by identifying the kind of benefit that would actually matter to them, and then ask a question that helps bring that into focus. If we skip this, we could accidentally be reinforcing organizational compliance instead of genuine ownership. Below are three common categories of benefits. There are many ways to make a change feel worth it, but these will get you started.

- **Student impact**
  Ask: "How could this genuinely help your students?"
  Deepen: "What would you hope to see your students doing differently if this really worked?"
- **Meaningful growth**
  Ask: "How could this stretch you in a way that feels meaningful?"
  Deepen: "What would make this feel like it strengthened your practice?"
- **Solving a real problem**
  Ask: "How could this make something easier or better in your room?"
  Deepen: "What current frustration could this help address?"

This is where motivation starts to form because they can see themselves in the payoff.

Coaching Guidance

You don't need to ask every question. Focus on listening first.

Ask what helps you understand which of the three drivers would help build value:

- What matters
- The cost
- What would make it worth it

Follow their thinking, not your script.

In the Field: Building the Skill of Listening for Value

Once you start listening through a Value Mindset lens, your attention changes. You start to hear more than what teachers say and begin to notice what feels worth their time and effort.

In some of my work with the Mississippi State Department of Education, I saw this play out in real time. Regional Coordinators, who support literacy coaches across the state, began adjusting how they listened in coaching conversations. Instead of responding to surface-level concerns, they started paying attention to what teachers were revealing about what felt worth their time, what felt risky, and what didn't yet feel meaningful.

That small change in attention started to show up in bigger ways. After working on this, one of the coordinators took it a step further and created what she called "coaching clinics," where her coaches practiced with real scenarios. They listened for the value, the risk, and the hesitation underneath the words, not just what was on the surface.

Over time, you could hear the difference. Instead of just responding to what was said, coaches were responding to what was driving it.

The Value Tool in Action

Scenario

A district is pushing more student discourse and less direct instruction.

A teacher says, "I've tried that before. It turns into chaos. My kids need structure."

Pause. This is a signal that something important feels at risk.

Step 1: Find out what matters to them.

Coach: "Okay. Tell me more. What feels most important to you here?"

Teacher: "I just don't want things to fall apart. When it gets loud, I lose control of the room."

Coach: "So keeping the room structured and calm matters a lot to you."

Teacher: "Yes. If it gets chaotic, they don't learn. And then it's on me."

Now we see it. What matters:

- Structure
- Student learning
- Professional responsibility

This is about protection.

Step 2: Investigate what it might cost.

Coach: "What worries you most about trying it again?"

Teacher: "That I'll look like I don't know what I'm doing. And honestly… it stresses me out."

There it is. The cost:

* Competence
* Reputation
* Emotional energy

Coach: "That makes sense. No one wants to feel out of control in their own room."

The teacher exhales. The focus turns from persuading to understanding.

Step 3: Discover what would make it worth it.

Coach: "If you were going to try something like this again, what would need to happen for it to feel worth it?"

Teacher: "It would have to actually help them think more. Not just talk more. And I'd need a way to keep it from getting out of control."

Coach: "So if you could see them thinking more deeply, and you had some guardrails to keep it structured, that would feel different?"

Teacher: "Yeah. That would feel different."

What Just Happened

Let's slow that down. Here's what actually changed in that moment:

* What she cared about was respected.

- Her risk was acknowledged.
- Her payoff became visible.

The coach did not try any of these moves:

- Argue research
- Remind her of expectations
- Say "Just try it"
- Minimize the fear

Any of those moves would have pulled the conversation back into compliance culture. The teacher would have defended harder, disengaged, or complied without commitment.

Instead, the coach built value.

The Coaching Shift

Resistance often sounds like this: "This won't work." or "I don't have time."

Underneath these statements are these beliefs:

- "I don't want to lose what matters."
- "This feels risky."
- "I don't see how this helps me."

When you address those three things, resistance starts to diminish. It starts to lessen as understanding deepens.

The coach helped her answer three internal questions:

- Does this honor what matters to me?
- What might this cost me?
- What would make this worthwhile?

Now, and only now, can the conversation move to strategy.

Use It Tomorrow

Listen for the resistance signals:

* "I don't really see how this helps my students."
* "This just isn't worth the time it's going to take."
* "I'm not against it. I just don't see the point."

Don't jump straight to strategy. Start here:

* Find out what matters to them.
* Understand what it might cost.
* Identify what would make it worth it.

Stay there long enough for the real answers to surface because that's where value starts forming.

Summary

At its core, the Value Mindset is about whether a change feels personally meaningful or merely required. When educators resist here, it often signals a disconnect. It is because the work does not yet connect to what they care about, what they are trying to protect, or who they believe themselves to be.

This chapter showed how easily schools fall into Compliance Culture, unintentionally training people to work for expectations, monitoring, or approval rather than purpose. Over time, that approach erodes commitment and weakens ownership.

Value is built through connection. It grows when we listen for what matters, name the real costs people perceive, and connect the work to motivations that already exist. When people can see how a change aligns with what they care about, engagement becomes more natural and more sustained.

Reflection Questions

1. How will I intentionally uncover what this educator already values rather than leading with what I want them to value?
2. What would need to happen for this change to feel worthwhile to this educator, and how will I help them articulate that in our conversation?
3. What is one concrete move I will make to surface and name the costs they may be dealing with, so the value of this change feels real, not just required?

Bonus Resources

The **V.A.L.U.E. Coaching Process** is a coaching method designed to support the Value Mindset.

Access this and other bonus resources at

www.thewholeeducator.com/book-resources

Chapter 5:
Belonging Mindset

"That Won't Work for These Kids"

"That won't work for these kids," Ms. F said, leaning back in her chair. Every coaching conversation seemed to land there. I'd been working with her for a few months, observing lessons, offering feedback, and still, nothing was moving. She was confident in her teaching and genuinely believed things were going well. She even wondered out loud if my time might be better spent supporting other teachers.

Her classroom looked calm on the surface. Students were compliant, lessons ran smoothly, but many of her English Language Learners were working on tasks that were lowered several grade levels. They were finishing the work, but they were not being stretched. When we explored next steps, she couldn't identify what she might change and she seldom saw value in my ideas. "That won't work for these kids," she'd repeat. As I worked with her, it became clear that she didn't trust that I respected her as a professional or understood her students well enough to offer strategies that would actually work in her classroom.

I kept trying to persuade, offering strategies and pushing for improvement. The more I pushed, the more stuck we both became. Our conversations felt like a quiet standoff. She was protecting her classroom and I was trying to improve it, neither of us getting anywhere.

It was honestly frustrating for both of us. The conversations felt heavy and unproductive, like we were spending time without actually moving anything forward.

So one day, I stopped.

I stopped trying to win the argument and prove that my strategy would work. Instead, I got curious. I asked her what she loved about teaching, when she felt most proud of her students, and what she worried people didn't understand about her classroom.

I listened, shifting out of my usual habit of listening to respond and focused fully on understanding her perspective.

As I leaned into understanding her perspective, she shared that her student Jose had melted down earlier in the year when given an on-level assignment, and in that moment she felt like she had completely lost control of the class. As she shared this very human moment, the tension started to dissipate. She shared more about the challenges her students faced and the moments when she felt proud of the progress they were making.

From there, we started exploring ideas together, possibilities we were both curious about. Eventually, we landed on a strategy she was excited to try.

During our next visit, she was beaming. The lesson worked. Students were engaged in ways they hadn't been before. She started to see what they were capable of and what she was capable of supporting.

From that point on, our coaching conversations changed. She became more open to trying new strategies and more willing to hear feedback about raising expectations.

What made the difference was understanding what she needed at that moment. Before she was ready to be helped, she needed to feel heard.

She needed to know that I respected her professional judgment and understood what she was trying to do for her students.

Belonging came before improvement.

The work didn't move when I pushed harder. It moved when I changed how she experienced me. When people feel respected and understood, they stop protecting themselves. Once that happens, growth becomes possible.

The Mindset: Belonging

Belonging isn't about being nice. It's about trust, connection, and safety.

People put their energy where they feel they belong. When that feeling weakens, or never develops, people don't necessarily leave the organization, but they begin protecting themselves. They hold back, take fewer risks, and only engage as much as feels safe.

The belief underneath the Belonging Mindset is simple:

I believe I belong here.

Think about walking into a new gym. If you walk in and feel judged, ignored, or out of place, it's hard to stay motivated. When someone greets you, shows you how things work, and treats you like you're part of the community, everything changes. You show up more consistently because you feel like you belong there.

The same thing happens in schools.

Belonging grows from three Belonging Conditions working together:

Trust + Connection + Safety = Belonging

Trust means people believe in both your character and competence. In his fantastic book, *The Speed of Trust*, Stephen M. R. Covey describes trust as the confidence we have in someone's integrity, intent, capabilities, and results. When people trust a leader or coach, they believe that person genuinely wants them to succeed and can actually help them get there.

Connection forms when people feel understood and respected. Research on interpersonal communication shows that when someone feels deeply understood, their brain activity begins to synchronize with the person listening. Scientists call this *neural entrainment*. It is the biological signal that connection is happening.

Safety is the belief that it is safe to be honest. Amy Edmondson's research on psychological safety found that teams learn and improve faster when people feel comfortable asking questions, admitting mistakes, and sharing ideas without fear of embarrassment or punishment.

These three conditions work together to create belonging.

When teachers trust the people around them, feel understood as professionals, and believe it is safe to speak honestly, they are far more willing to engage, learn, and grow.

When any of these conditions weaken, belonging starts to fade.

When belonging fades, resistance often appears.

Why Leaders Struggle to Support This Mindset

Most leaders believe they are creating belonging, but what often gets reinforced is politeness. The challenge is that belonging is easy to misunderstand.

We focus on creating positive cultures and emphasize professionalism, collegiality, and polite protocols. Meetings stay respectful, and people are encouraged to collaborate and treat one another well.

Those intentions matter, but belonging grows from more than a positive tone.

Belonging grows when people trust one another, feel recognized as professionals, and believe it is safe to speak honestly about their work.

Two leadership habits often get in the way:

First, we are trained to move conversations forward. When someone raises a concern or uncertainty, our instinct is to clarify the plan, explain the reasoning, or offer advice. These responses feel efficient and practical, but we can unintentionally move the conversation past the moment when someone was trying to be understood.

I call this *efficiency bias*: the leadership instinct to move quickly to solutions instead of slowing down to understand what someone is really trying to say. Ironically, this attempt to save time often backfires.

I was caught in this very bias with Ms. F. At the time, I supported several teachers each day. I felt pressure to keep our conversation moving so I could get to the next classroom.

I thought the faster I explained the strategy, the faster we could move forward. However, when people don't feel understood, the concern keeps resurfacing, and the conversation stretches longer than it would have if we had paused to listen in the first place.

Second, we often interpret smooth conversations as a sign that belonging is strong. When meetings feel calm and disagreements are rare, it may seem like the culture is working. However, belonging isn't measured by how comfortable conversations feel. It's revealed by whether educators feel safe enough to be honest about what's actually happening in their classrooms or on their campuses.

When those conditions are missing, educators often protect themselves in subtle ways. They share less openly, ask fewer questions, keep concerns to themselves, or only talk about things that are going well.

Over time, we start to see signs of resistance without realizing the relational conditions that support belonging have weakened.

The Silent Progress Blocker: Culture of Niceness

Everyone's kind, everyone's smiling, and no one wants to rock the boat. On the surface, it feels safe. Underneath, the culture of niceness is silently working against the very progress we so desperately want to make. Like painting over a wall full of cracks, it looks fine until you lean on it.

The reality is, in many schools, we've mistaken politeness for belonging. Niceness protects comfort, and belonging builds courage. Everyone's smiling, but few people are speaking honestly. When we prioritize being nice, we trade honesty for harmony. We may have fewer critical conversations, but we end up with more surface-level relationships and leaders who hesitate to challenge harmful practices because they don't want to ruffle feathers. Staffrooms, grade-level or department meetings, and professional development sessions stay polite but guarded. People smile through tension instead of addressing it. We mistake self-protection for agreement.

Here's the trap: leaders often think they're preserving peace when they avoid conflict. What they're really doing is eroding trust. Niceness might keep the peace in the short term, but it kills psychological safety in the long run. In a Culture of Niceness, people might feel comfortable but not safe because good intentions often hide a fear of vulnerability. Without vulnerability, trust struggles to grow. If honesty gets you iced out or labeled as "negative," safety has not been established.

In response to challenges, we often hear statements such as, "Kill them with kindness," "I don't want to ruffle feathers," or "It's not a big deal," when it's actually a motherload of a big deal.

This Culture of Niceness is the kryptonite of the Belonging Mindset because it rewards comfort over honesty, replaces authenticity with appearance, and buries the critical conversations our schools need most.

Belonging shows up when people can disagree and still feel accepted. If disagreement isn't safe, belonging isn't real.

A strong culture of belonging allows conflict without threatening the relationship, so when tension shows up, strong leaders lean in, instead of just patching over the cracks. They focus on building repair.

Belonging starts with trust because, until people can be honest, real connection isn't possible.

The Cost of Getting This Wrong

There is a real cost to glossing over a lack of belonging. The first mistake is confusing silence for trust, agreement, and safety when it actually signals withdrawal and protection. Coaches become the "safe people" for venting but not for growth because honesty with those in authority feels risky. Teachers close their doors, operate independently, and stop seeking help. They hesitate to take risks or try new approaches because they're unsure how mistakes will be received. Emotional energy drains from teams. People protect themselves instead of investing in each other.

Connection erodes when leaders stay in their heads instead of being present for the person in front of them. The biggest mistake is trying to "protocol" and "sentence stem" your way out of it. You hear it in the request: "Just give me what to say." The conversation becomes managed, loses its sense of meaning, and their protective shield stays up. I was doing exactly this with Ms. F, trying to steer the conversation instead of truly hearing her.

As Brené Brown reminds us, it's not fear that gets in the way of daring leadership. It's armor.

Over time, the ripple effects spread. Teachers stop bringing problems forward, innovation slows because risk feels unsafe, and new staff struggle to integrate. Veteran staff feel unseen and taken for granted, and coaching becomes more about growth to compliance. Leaders shoulder more and more of the emotional weight alone.

Commitment weakens because people don't feel connected to the people doing the work. When belonging is weak, people begin to withdraw in ways that are easy to miss and hard to recover from.

The Shift

So how do we begin strengthening belonging in our schools?

Stop focusing only on keeping people comfortable.

Start paying attention to the Belonging Conditions that allow people to be honest, heard, and respected.

Belonging builds over time through consistent experiences of trust, connection, and safety.

When resistance appears in coaching conversations, the question is not:

"How do I get them on board?"

The better question is:

"Which condition of belonging might be missing here?"

Once you can identify that, your next move becomes much clearer.

The Core Idea

Make them feel seen, safe, and supported.

The Practice

The Resistance Signal

When belonging is weak, resistance has a recognizable sound.

You might hear statements such as these from teachers:

- "I don't want to open that can of worms."
- "My team doesn't care what I think anyway."
- "I don't think anyone really sees how much we're juggling."
- "I've learned to just keep my head down."
- "When you speak up around here, it tends to backfire."

Sometimes the resistance sounds sharp, and other times it sounds guarded.

Underneath the words is often a quieter message:

- "I'm not sure I trust this."
- "I'm not sure you understand me."
- "I'm not sure it's safe to say what I really think."

When you hear language like this, don't rush to explain. This moment is about helping someone feel safe enough to stay in the conversation.

The Tool: The Belonging Lens

Before moving to strategy, pause and look at the situation through the **Belonging Lens**.

Ask yourself: **What part of belonging might be fragile right now?**

Most belonging breakdowns show up in one of three places:

- **Trust** – Do I trust you?
- **Connection** – Do you respect my perspective?
- **Safety** – Is it safe to be honest here?

How to Support Each Condition

Before moving to strategy, pause and look at the situation through the **Belonging Lens**.

Ask yourself:
What part of belonging might be fragile right now?

Belonging usually breaks down in three places.

Belonging Condition	The Question They Are Asking	Leadership Move

Trust	Do I trust you?	Be clear, consistent, and follow through.
Connection	Do you respect me as a professional?	Match the motive.
Safety	Is it safe to be honest here?	Acknowledge the risk.

Your job is to stay focused on what is happening in the interaction. Listen for which belonging question hasn't been answered yet. Once you recognize the question underneath the moment, you can respond in a way that strengthens belonging instead of pushing past it.

Trust

The question underneath the moment: *Do I trust your character and competence?*

In the *Speed of Trust*, Stephen M. R. Covey shares that trust is built through four core elements:

- Intent (character)
- Integrity (character)
- Capability (competence)
- Results (competence)

What the leader listens for:

Uncertainty about whether you:

- are genuinely trying to help them succeed (intent)
- will follow through on what you say (integrity)
- have the expertise to support them effectively (capability)
- can actually help them see progress with their students (results)

When trust is fragile, people often test credibility before they engage.

Leadership move: Strengthen the unsupported element of trust.

- If you hear the trust element of **intent**:
  Connect *your* purpose to outcomes that matter to *them*.
- If you hear the trust element of **integrity**:
  Do what you say you'll do. When you don't, acknowledge it and make it right.
- If you hear the trust element of **capabilities**:
  Demonstrate relevant expertise through modeling or co-planning.
- If you hear the trust element of **results**:
  Share examples of impact with similar students and situations.

Trust grows when people see evidence, not just encouragement.

Connection

The question underneath the moment: *Do you respect me as a professional and trust my judgment?*

Connection strengthens when educators feel their expertise and thinking are respected.

In conversation, people are usually looking for one of three things:

- **Hugged**: They need their effort or frustration acknowledged.
- **Heard**: They need their professional thinking understood.
- **Helped**: They need support solving a problem.

When the response doesn't match the motive, the conversation begins to break down.

What the leader listens for: Signals that the educator may be protecting their professional credibility before engaging.

Leadership move: Match the motive.

- If they need to be **hugged**:
  Acknowledge the emotion, effort and complexity of their work.
- If they need to be **heard**:
  Ask questions that help them explain their thinking.
- If they need to be **helped**:
  Collaborate on strategies or next steps.

Connection strengthens when people feel respected before their practice is challenged.

Safety

The question underneath the moment: *Is it safe to be honest here?*

Safety gets strengthened in the moment someone takes a risk.

Examples:

- disagreement
- admitting confusion
- questioning a plan
- sharing frustration

Leadership move: Acknowledge the honesty before moving to solutions.

- "I'm really glad you said that."
- "That's important."
- "Tell me more."

Safety grows when honesty leads to understanding instead of correction.

Coaching Guidance

You can stay effective without diagnosing belonging perfectly. You need to stay curious long enough to see what might be missing. Follow the conversation, not your script. Your role is to strengthen the Belonging Conditions that make honest learning possible.

The Belonging Lens Tool in Action

Scenario

A coach meets with Jordan, a veteran teacher, to discuss a new instructional strategy the school is encouraging teachers to try.

When the coach mentions the strategy, Jordan leans back in his chair, crosses his arms, and says:

"I've been teaching for twenty years. I know what works with my students."

Step 1: Observe.

The coach notices a few things:

- Jordan's body language becomes more guarded.

- The response is brief and defensive.
- Jordan does not ask any questions about the strategy.

These observations give partial information about what may be happening. They simply signal that **something in the relationship may need attention**.

Step 2: Listen for the belonging question.

The coach pauses and considers the Belonging Lens before moving into explanation or persuasion.

Which Belonging Condition might still be unsupported: trust, connection, or safety?

Jordan's response suggests the concern may be about **being recognized as a professional**. The coach considers the **connection** lens. Jordan may be wondering:

"Do you recognize my experience and respect my professional judgment?"

Step 3: Make a leadership move.

The coach decides to strengthen **connection** before discussing the strategy.

Instead of defending the idea, the coach responds:

"You've been doing this a long time. I'd love to hear more about what you've seen work best with this group."

Jordan relaxes slightly and begins explaining the challenges of the current class. As he talks, the coach listens carefully. This moment calls for **Heard**.

The coach asks: "What have you noticed about how they respond when discussions start to fizzle out?"

Jordan continues sharing observations and examples from the classroom.

After a few minutes, Jordan pauses and says: "I mean, I'm open to ideas. I just don't want to try something that wastes time."

Now the coach hears something different.

Jordan may be ready for **Helped**.

The coach responds: "Would it be helpful if we looked at one small way to try this strategy with that group?"

Jordan nods.

The conversation moves forward, not because the coach pushed harder, but because the coach first strengthened the Belonging Condition that was missing.

Connection opened the door for coaching.

What Just Happened

Belonging began forming as a result of several factors:

* The teacher felt understood.
* The relationship felt respectful.
* The risk of honesty decreased.

The coach did not do any of the following:

* Defend their expertise.
* Jump straight to solutions.
* Dismiss the concern.

Instead, the coach strengthened connection.

The Coaching Shift

Resistance often looks like disagreement or silence, but underneath it is often a belonging question:

* Do I trust you?
* Do you respect me?
* Is it safe to be honest here?

When those questions are answered, resistance reduces on its own because the relationship makes learning helpful and safe.

Use It Tomorrow

Listen for belonging signals:

* "I've been doing this a long time."
* "My team doesn't care what I think anyway."
* "It's fine." (when it's not)

Before offering solutions, pause and ask yourself:

* Is this a trust gap?
* Is this a connection gap?
* Is this a safety gap?

Then respond to the Belonging Condition before moving to strategy.

That is where belonging begins.

Summary

The Belonging Mindset reflects whether educators feel accepted, supported, safe, and respected within the professional community around them. When resistance shows up here, it signals uncertainty about the relationship surrounding the work.

This chapter showed how easily schools can confuse harmony with belonging. When leaders prioritize keeping interactions comfortable, conversations may remain polite while important perspectives remain unspoken. Over time, educators may protect their credibility, limit what they share, and quietly disengage from conversations that require honesty or vulnerability.

Belonging develops through more than friendly interactions. It develops when educators consistently experience three conditions in their relationships: trust in the people leading the work, recognition of their professional judgment, and confidence that honest dialogue will not threaten the relationship. When those conditions are present, conversations become more genuine, collaboration deepens, and educators are far more willing to participate in learning and change.

Reflection Questions

1. Which part of belonging might need attention in this coaching relationship right now: trust, connection or safety?
2. Where might trust be breaking down across intent, integrity, capability, or results, and what would rebuild it?
3. Does this teacher need to feel hugged, heard, or helped right now, and how will I respond in a way that shows I respect their professional expertise?
4. What is one way I can invite more honest dialogue, so this educator feels comfortable sharing what they truly think or need?

You're not alone in this. Every leader is learning, practicing, and rebuilding trust, connection and safety in real time (including me). The difference is that now you know *where to start*.

When belonging is in place, people stop protecting themselves and start engaging in the work.

Bonus Resources

The Trust Map, Seeking Questions, and **The Risk Response** are tools designed to support the Belonging Mindset.

Access these and other bonus resources at **thewholeeducator.com/book-resources**.

Chapter 6: Success Mindset

"I Can't Make Them Learn"

"I can't make them learn if they don't want to." She didn't say it dramatically. It came out flat, like something she'd repeated enough times that it no longer felt worth questioning.

Her coach and I had just finished observing her class. Students sat behind glowing screens while she moved through the lesson from the front of the room. When independent work began, several drifted right back to their devices. The teacher walked to the back of the classroom, rolled her eyes, and sighed. "See? I can never get them to do anything."

The coach and I exchanged a quick glance. We'd both seen this before.

This wasn't the first time we'd been in this teacher's classroom. She and the coach had been working together all year in observation and feedback cycles focused on behavior management. They had tried things. All year, they'd been adjusting, reflecting, and trying new strategies. On paper, it looked like the kind of steady coaching that should lead somewhere.

And yet, here we were.

Later, I asked how she thought the lesson went. She didn't hesitate. "I can't make them learn if they don't want to." Then I asked what she wanted to work on next.

"Behavior management."

From her perspective, the problem was clear. If she could manage them better, learning would follow. I remember sitting with that. It would have been easy to stay there, to simply offer another strategy. What I heard underneath her words sounded like defeat.

Somewhere along the way, she had stopped believing she could be successful. She had tried and had worked hard, but nothing meaningful came of it. When effort keeps showing up without results, something deeper starts to erode: her belief that her effort will pay off.

The following week, I returned. The behavior hadn't changed. For a moment, I caught myself thinking about the next strategy, and then I paused. She didn't need another behavior management strategy.

Midway through the lesson, I leaned in and asked, "Can I offer a suggestion that might help?" She nodded. I shared a small adjustment that she tried immediately.

At first, only a few students responded, but as a few more began to join in, the directions started to make sense and small conversations formed around the task. The energy in the room shifted in a way you could feel, slowly but noticeably, as the noise that once felt distracting started to sound more like learning taking hold.

The next morning, I got an email: "Yesterday was the best day I've ever had here."

All the planning, encouragement, and feedback conversations hadn't shifted her belief, yet that one small moment did, as she saw something work in a way that hadn't happened before. In that experience, belief began to grow, and in the same classroom, with the same students, her sense of what was possible started to change.

That belief is the foundation of the Success Mindset.

The Mindset: Success

People put in effort when they believe they can be successful. When that belief fades, so does the effort.

The belief underneath the Success Mindset is simple:

** I believe I can be successful. **

Think about someone starting a new workout routine. If they go to the gym for weeks and never feel stronger or see progress, motivation drops quickly. It becomes easy to assume, "Maybe I'm just not someone who can do this." The moment they notice even a small sign of progress, lifting a little more weight or finishing a workout that used to feel impossible, something changes. The effort suddenly feels worthwhile because success starts to feel possible.

The same dynamic shows up in schools.

The Success Mindset is rooted in what researchers call self-efficacy, the belief that our actions can produce the results we're aiming for. Psychologist Albert Bandura's work showed that people persist longer, try harder, and recover faster from setbacks when they believe success is within reach.

That belief develops over time through experience. In schools, it grows from two conditions working together:

Outcome Clarity + Attainability Belief = Success Mindset

Outcome Clarity means people understand what success actually looks like. If the goal is fuzzy, improvement becomes guesswork.

One of my favorite questions to ask a school leader is: *"If I asked all of your teachers what good teaching looks like here, would their answers sound similar?"*

If the answers vary widely, the destination isn't clear. When the destination isn't clear, people end up navigating improvement on their own.

Attainability Belief means that once people understand the goal, they believe they can actually reach it. Do they believe they can influence student learning? Do they believe their efforts can lead to better outcomes? Do they believe the strategies in front of them will work with their students?

This is where belief either strengthens or quietly breaks down.

Research consistently shows that the strongest source of self-efficacy is **mastery experience**: seeing our actions lead to success. When people can connect their effort to a visible result, belief grows. When progress is hard to see, even hardworking educators begin to question whether their efforts are making a difference.

When people understand what success looks like and believe it's possible for them to achieve it, the Success Mindset is present.

Why Leaders Struggle to Support This Mindset

One of the hardest moments for leaders happens when a teacher says something such as, "My kids can't do it."

For many leaders, that statement is a red flag. It sounds like low expectations. It can feel like the teacher is giving up on students or choosing a path that moves away from growth. Leaders care deeply about what students are capable of, so the instinct is to respond quickly.

We push back on the belief, remind the teacher that all students can learn, and share examples of other classrooms where the strategy is working. Sometimes we reinforce expectations or introduce new instructional approaches that might help the teacher move forward.

All of those responses are understandable. They come from a desire to protect rigor and advocate for students. In that moment, leaders are often responding to what the statement sounds like and missing what it actually represents.

When a teacher says, "My kids can't do it," they are often revealing something about their own experience. They have tried strategies, put in effort, and have not seen the results they hoped for. Over time, those experiences shape what they believe is possible in their classroom. From the inside, that belief *feels* grounded and realistic.

This is where leaders can unintentionally get stuck. We try to change belief through persuasion. We explain why a strategy *should* work or why a goal matters. Sometimes we offer encouragement, hoping confidence will follow. However, belief in success hardly ever grows from persuasion or encouragement. **It grows from experience.**

When educators see their actions lead to a small, visible success, something starts to change. The story they have been telling themselves about what is possible begins to fade. Confidence builds as they see the evidence for themselves.

Without those visible moments of success, even dedicated educators can start to question their impact. When belief weakens, effort eventually follows.

The Silent Progress Blocker: Progress Ambiguity

A leader stops by a classroom and later sits down with the teacher to reflect on the lesson.

"I'd love to see more engagement in this lesson," the leader says.

The teacher agrees. Over the next few weeks, they try new strategies. They add discussion, experiment with different activities, and adjust their pacing.

When the leader returns and asks how engagement is improving, the teacher pauses.

"I'm not really sure."

The leader wants to help. The teacher wants to improve. Neither can see progress.

This happens in schools more often than we realize. Leaders ask teachers to improve things such as engagement, differentiation, or student ownership. These are important goals, but they are also big and blurry. When the goal is that broad, progress is hard to see. Self-efficacy grows from seeing your effort work.

In many schools, progress is trapped inside what I call the **too big, too blurry** approach to improvement. A teacher tries to improve engagement (too big), where one lesson feels a little better, another feels messy, and the next lands somewhere in between. Without a clear way to see progress (too blurry), success becomes a matter of interpretation and loses clarity in observation. When success is subjective, the Success Mindset never fully takes hold.

This is where mastery experience starts to break down. Earlier, we talked about how belief grows when people can see their effort lead to success. That only works when success is visible. In many schools, it isn't.

When goals are too big or results remain untracked, that connection breaks. The brain never receives the signal it needs: *I did this, and it worked.*

Without that loop of **action → evidence → belief**, even hardworking educators begin to question their impact. They invest energy into improvement, but because success is difficult to see, it feels like nothing is changing.

This is what **progress ambiguity** looks like.

When progress isn't clear, a different thought starts to creep in: I'm not sure what I'm doing is actually helping.

Confidence grows when progress becomes visible. Small, clear wins enable teachers to see that their actions are making a difference. You cannot build confidence in something you cannot see yourself succeeding at.

The Cost of Getting This Wrong

When belief in success weakens, the effects ripple through effort, instruction, coaching, and leadership. Progress starts to fade when people keep trying but don't believe it will make a difference. Teachers don't believe the goal is attainable, so they disengage before they even start. "These kids can't do it" becomes the operating belief shaping instruction. You hear comments such as, "My students just aren't ready for that yet," or "I've tried that before, and it didn't really work."

Setbacks are interpreted as proof the outcome isn't possible, and the opportunity for feedback gets missed. Initiative fatigue increases because educators don't see results tied to effort.

Rigor erodes as expectations lower. Students experience watered-down instruction because adults no longer believe success is realistic. Teachers spend time venting about student behavior and learning gaps, and they infrequently seek coaching because they question whether it will lead to real improvement. They say things such as, "I feel like I've tried." Coaches spend more time convincing than coaching because belief in success is missing. They begin triaging who they invest in, assuming some educators or teams just won't get there.

Data conversations feel defeating and lose their sense of support. Teachers become defensive, and results are explained away instead of used to plan next moves. Leaders work hard to provide supportive strategies while belief in the outcome remains the underlying barrier. Time and energy go into new tools, and confidence in what is possible remains underdeveloped. Accountability feels punitive because success feels out of reach. If people don't believe success is possible, they stop truly trying.

The Shift

So how do we start to build a sense of success for our staff when implementing change?

Stop assuming effort alone will build confidence. When teachers try something new and can't see whether it worked, doubt grows. Conversations become, "My students just aren't ready for this," or "I've tried that before, and it didn't work."

Start helping teachers experience visible progress. Break large goals into small instructional moves that can be tested, observed, and reflected on. When educators can see the connection between their actions and student learning, belief begins to grow.

Confidence grows from evidence.

When teachers see that something they tried actually worked, even in a small way, their brain updates the story it tells about what kind of success is possible because they experienced it.

The Core Idea

Help them see evidence they can succeed.

The Practice

The Resistance Signal

In real time, this form of resistance has a recognizable sound. You might hear teachers say:

- "My kids can't do it."
- "I don't know if I can do this."
- "They're too far behind for this to work."
- "I've tried this before and it didn't work."
- "I'm just not very good at this kind of thing."

When you hear language like this, it is important to pause rather than react. The instinct in these moments is often to push encouragement, offer quick solutions, or reassure them that they'll be fine. Most of us have been trained to do exactly that. This is usually a Success Mindset problem.

The coaching cue is simple, but not always easy: slow down and build belief. Before offering solutions, consider what evidence they have, what experiences may have shaped their confidence, and what support would help them see a path forward. Moving too quickly to encouragement can feel empty. Staying in curiosity helps you understand what's getting in the way of their belief.

The Tool: 3E Success Conditions

Success Mindset grows from three conditions.

3E Success Conditions

EXPOSURE   ENVIRONMENT   EVIDENCE

- **Exposure:** Seeing someone like me succeed
- **Environment:** Feeling supported and safe enough to try
- **Evidence:** Experiencing real success from my own effort

These three conditions reinforce the two elements that create the Success Mindset:

- **Exposure** → builds **outcome clarity.**
- **Environment** → creates psychological safety.
- **Evidence** → builds **attainability belief**.

When these three conditions are present, belief begins to grow. When one or more of these conditions are missing, even hardworking teachers begin to doubt that improvement is possible. When belief starts to weaken, leaders can begin with a simple question:

Which of these conditions might need support right now?

Exposure

Seeing someone like me succeed.

People believe something is possible when they see someone like them do it, not the superstar or the teacher of the year. The normal human with similar students, schedule, and constraints.

Observing someone else succeed does two important things: it makes the outcome feel possible, and it helps teachers see what success looks like in practice.

Leaders can support exposure in the following ways:

- **Invite teachers to observe a peer implementing the change.** In this way, they can see what the practice looks like in a real classroom with similar students and constraints.
- **Share short video clips of classroom practice.** This enables teachers to see concrete examples of the strategy in action and begin visualizing how it might look in their classroom.
- **Model a strategy.** Have teachers or the coach model a strategy during team meetings or live in the classroom so others can see it in action, talk through how it works, and consider how they might try it with their own students.

Exposure works best when teachers have time to reflect on what they observed. Without that reflection, success can easily be explained away as luck or "having the good kids."

Seeing it makes success feel possible.

Environment

Feeling supported and safe enough to try.

Trying something new always carries risk. If the environment feels judgmental, rushed, or overwhelming, people become far less willing to experiment. Belief grows when teachers feel supported enough to try, adjust, and try again.

Leaders can strengthen the environment by doing the following:

- **Give feedback that summarizes three questions.** What is the goal? (Feed Up), How am I doing? (Feed Back), What should I try next? (Feed Forward)
- **Help teachers emotionally regulate difficult moments.** Research shows that accurately naming what someone is feeling in the moment can help the brain begin to regulate. It helps to acknowledge the challenge or emotion behind the experience ("That looked like a tough moment"), point out one thing that worked, and narrow the next step to something small enough to try again tomorrow.
- **Encourage collaboration and shared problem-solving.** This can be done through co-planning lessons, having teachers observing each other's classrooms, examining student work together, and talking honestly about what is working and what still feels hard.

When the risk feels manageable, people are far more willing to try again.

Evidence

Experiencing real success from my own effort.

The most powerful way to grow a person's belief in success is by *experiencing* the evidence that success is possible. Teachers need opportunities to try something new and see it work, even in a small way.

Leaders can help teachers build evidence by doing the following:

- **Break large goals into manageable "micro-movements."** These small actions can be tested and observed, so teachers can try one small change, see what happens, and begin connecting their actions to visible results.

- **Provide in-the-moment guidance.** This is sometimes called whisper coaching, quietly offering brief suggestions during a lesson, such as prompting a teacher to wait a few more seconds, ask a follow-up question, or try a specific move. This in-the-moment coaching enables them to adjust in real time and immediately see the impact of the change.

- **Reflect with teachers to connect the outcome to their own actions.** You can ask questions such as, "What did you do there that helped that work?" so they can see how their instructional decisions influenced the result.

These small moments matter because they turn effort into visible proof. When teachers see that something they tried changed what students did, the brain registers it as evidence: *I did something that worked.* That evidence is what strengthens belief. Success Mindset grows when educators can clearly see the connection between what they did and what happened next.

Choosing the Right Support

Ask yourself: *What is missing right now: clarity, safety, or proof?*

* Clarity → Exposure
* Safety → Environment
* Proof → Evidence

If teachers lack **Clarity** and cannot see what success looks like: Create **Exposure**.

If they lack **Safety** and feel alone, overwhelmed, or defensive: Strengthen the **Environment**.

If they lack **Proof** that their effort has led to visible results: Help them see **Evidence** of success.

Success Mindset grows in our classrooms and on our campuses when educators experience success for themselves. One of the most important things leaders can do is help design that first win.

**You can't talk someone into believing they can do it.
They have to experience it.**

The 3E Success Conditions Tool In Action

Scenario

Marisol, a fifth grade ELA teacher, had been working on improving student writing stamina for weeks. The coach had been observing lessons and offering feedback around modeling, pacing, and directions.

Marisol was open and reflective, but nothing was changing. Students still shut down quickly, and Marisol stepped in to rescue them.

During one debrief she admitted, "I know what I'm supposed to do. I just don't think it's going to work with this group."

Pause.

This is a signal that belief in success is starting to weaken.

Marisol understood the strategy. She just didn't believe the outcome was attainable.

Step 1: Identify the missing condition.

The coach paused to consider the three conditions that support the Success Mindset:

- Exposure
- Environment
- Evidence

Marisol already had exposure. She had seen the strategy modeled and had discussed it in coaching conversations.

The environment was supportive. She felt safe reflecting and trying new approaches. What was missing was **evidence**. She had not experienced a moment where the strategy worked with *her* students.

Step 2: Create a small opportunity for evidence.

The coach asked if she could partner with Marisol during writing time the next day.

During the lesson, the coach sat beside her and quietly whisper-coached as the writing block unfolded.

When students hesitated, the coach prompted Marisol to wait a few seconds longer before stepping in. When a student started writing, the coach encouraged her to narrate the effort instead of correcting.

Slowly, more students began writing. One asked for another page. Writing time lasted longer than it had all month.

Step 3: Reflect on the evidence.

After class, Marisol looked surprised. "That actually worked."

Instead of offering more feedback, the coach asked a simple question: "What did you do there that helped that work?"

Marisol paused. "I didn't rescue them… and they didn't fall apart." Then she smiled and said with a spark of hope, "Maybe they can do this. Maybe I can help them get there."

What Just Happened

Marisol needed more than a new strategy. She specifically needed a moment where the strategy worked.

Up until that point, the coaching had focused on what to do. What was missing was an experience that showed her it could actually work with her students. The coach didn't just explain the strategy again. She stayed in the moment, supported Marisol through the discomfort, and helped create a small win in real time.

That moment became evidence, and it began to shift Marisol's belief about what was possible for her students and for herself.

The Coaching Shift

When teachers begin to doubt success is possible, leaders often respond with more instruction: more strategies, more accountability, or more feedback. When belief is missing, those moves lead to real change.

The coach changed their thinking from, "What should she do better?" to "Which condition is missing?"

Then she designed a moment where Marisol could experience success for herself. That small moment of evidence began to rebuild belief.

Use It Tomorrow

Listen for the signals that the Belief Mindset needs strengthening:

- "My students just aren't ready for that yet."
- "I've tried that before, and it didn't really work."
- "I don't think this will work with this group."

Don't jump straight to new strategies. Start here:

- Help them see what success looks like.
- Create a small opportunity to try.
- Look together for what worked.

If you stay there long enough for the evidence to show up, belief in success starts to grow.

Summary

The Success Mindset is the belief that success is possible and that our actions can influence the outcome. In schools, that belief grows when two conditions are present: educators are clear what success looks like (outcome clarity), and they believe it is attainable for them (attainability belief). When either condition is missing, effort begins to fade as belief in impact weakens.

One of the most common barriers to this mindset is progress ambiguity. When goals are too big or too blurry, teachers cannot clearly see whether their efforts are working. Without visible progress, even hardworking educators begin to question their impact.

Leaders build the Success Mindset by helping educators experience small, visible wins. Belief grows when three conditions are present: teachers can see what success looks like (exposure), they feel supported enough to try (environment), and they experience real proof that their efforts make a difference (evidence). When these conditions are in place, educators begin to see the connection between their actions and student learning. When teachers see that something they tried actually worked, belief begins to grow.

Reflection Questions

1. Where in my school might teachers be working hard but struggling to see clear evidence that their efforts are making a difference?

2. When a teacher says something such as, "My students can't do it," how do I usually respond, and how might I help them experience a small success instead?

3. Which of the three drivers of the Success Mindset might be missing right now for the educators I support: exposure, environment, or evidence?

Bonus Resources

The **Success Coaching Map** is an expanded tool that includes additional supports and strategies for the 3E Success Conditions, along with guidance for when to use each one. Access this and other bonus resources at **thewholeeducator.com/book-resources**.

Plans are necessary.

Praise helps.

But confidence comes from seeing it work.

Chapter 7:
Growth Mindset

The Feedback That Went Nowhere

"It was a nice review," she'd say with a shrug. I was coaching a coach in Florida who was considered one of the best in her district. She had years of experience, strong relationships, and a lot of credibility with teachers. I was leading professional learning, modeling coaching, and debriefing with her each visit.

Every time I asked what she'd learned, she said the same thing: "It was a nice review."

Month after month, nothing changed.

I had observed enough to know she needed the very skills we were practicing: asking reflective questions, holding the pause, and letting teachers think instead of jumping in with advice. But our debriefs stayed surface level. Eventually I started to feel like I was wasting her time, so I tried harder. I changed the structure, brought new examples, and adjusted the activities. Still nothing changed.

A story started forming in my mind: this coach was arrogant, set in her ways, and one of those coaches who thinks they already know everything. I didn't say any of this out loud, but I started believing it. The more I believed it, the more my behavior changed.

Our sessions became tighter and more structured. I started showing up with agendas, forms, and documentation. If she wasn't going to grow, at least I could prove I had done my part. Those are natural moves when you think someone isn't willing to learn. The truth is, that belief came from my frustration.

One day after another flat debrief, I stopped and did a quick internal audit. *Where might I be contributing to this?* There it was. I had lost my Growth Mindset *about her.* I had decided she wasn't going to change. Once I made that decision, I started coaching her like someone who wouldn't.

The next time I visited, I committed to focusing on a Growth Mindset about her: *What if she could change? If she wasn't arrogant or dismissive, what else might be happening?*

I started paying closer attention, and during a coaching conversation she was leading that day, I noticed something new.

The approach I had been teaching, the reflective questions, pauses, and uncertainty, asked her to step out of the expert role she had mastered. It required her to let teachers think out loud, even when the conversation wandered a little.

That kind of coaching is powerful, but it's also vulnerable. Once I saw that, I started approaching things differently. I stopped tightening the structure and trying to hold her accountable to the strategy. I started supporting her while she practiced the skill.

Before her coaching conversations, we role-played the uncomfortable moments: the pauses, the wandering thinking, and the urge to jump in with advice. I also gave her a few simple question stems she could glance at if she felt herself slipping back into advice. We treated the approach as practice rather than immediate mastery.

Suddenly she had a lot to reflect on after our sessions. She started naming what felt hard, what she noticed, and what she wanted to try next. Soon she was sharing her learning with other coaches and experimenting with the very strategies she had once brushed off as "just a review."

The turning point was a mindset shift. My lack of a Growth Mindset had kept me from seeing what she needed. The moment I stopped labeling her limitations and started supporting her development, her willingness opened.

Growth Mindset is something we practice when we're frustrated with the very people we're trying to help grow.

The Mindset: Growth

The belief underneath the Growth Mindset is simple:

I believe I can improve.

It is not working hard.
Not trying your best.
Not being positive.
Not resilience.
Not praising effort.

Those are *outcomes* of a Growth Mindset, not the mindset itself.

Growth Mindset is a belief you hold, not an action you perform. When someone believes improvement is possible, they stay engaged in the learning process longer, seek feedback, and keep working through confusion and frustration instead of avoiding it. Growth Mindset shows up when someone stays in the discomfort of learning long enough to grow.

Somewhere along the way, this idea became misunderstood in schools. In many schools, Growth Mindset has been reduced to slogans. Posters went up, and phrases like "not yet" started showing up everywhere, but often without a clear path forward. Students were told their brains could grow, but that message wasn't consistently connected to how we designed learning or supported progress. Effort without progress doesn't build belief in growth. Growth Mindset is the belief that improvement is possible while someone is still figuring things out. That belief develops through practice, not encouragement alone.

This is where Growth Mindset often gets confused with the Success Mindset.

> Success says, *I can succeed at this*.
> Growth says, *I can get better at this*, especially when it's messy.

Why Leaders Struggle to Support This Mindset

We encourage reflection, talk about learning from mistakes, and ask teachers to try new approaches. We genuinely want educators to grow.

The challenge is that the systems we lead often pull us in a different direction.

Classroom visits are tied to observation cycles, feedback is connected to rubrics and performance indicators, and new instructional practices are introduced and then quickly monitored for implementation fidelity. None of these structures are inherently wrong. Evaluation and accountability are necessary parts of schooling, but they create tension for leaders.

When time is limited and accountability pressure is high, it is natural to lean on structures already built into the system. Observation checklists, walkthrough data, and fidelity checks become the primary way improvement is monitored because those tools and routines are available.

Without realizing it, the focus quietly drifts from learning to getting it right.

Silent Progress Blocker: Learning–Performance Confusion

In many schools, teachers get nervous when they are observed. They need things to look polished during coaching conversations and are uncomfortable taking risks and experimentation. This often happens when the line between the Learning Zone and the Performance Zone becomes unclear:

In the **Learning Zone**, the goal is improvement. People are practicing, revising, experimenting, and building new capacity. Mistakes are expected because they are part of learning.

In the **Performance Zone**, the goal is execution. People apply what they already know how to do. Reliability matters and results are evaluated.

In his book *The Performance Paradox*, Eduardo Briceño describes that people move between these two zones when developing a skill. When educators aren't sure which zone they are in, the experience of learning begins to change: practice starts to feel like evaluation, feedback starts to feel like judgment, and struggle starts to look like evidence that someone isn't competent.

When that happens, teachers do something very human: they protect their sense of competence. They stick with strategies they already know, polish lessons before trying them publicly, and hesitate to ask for help. From the outside, it can look like teachers are unwilling to grow. The real issue sits in the culture. The environment has made struggle feel risky.

Without zone clarity, the message becomes confusing. Mistakes are "welcome" until they show up in evaluation. Risk-taking is "encouraged" until results are expected immediately. When that happens, schools lose the safety to struggle, which is exactly what learning requires.

The Cost of Getting This Wrong

When the environment doesn't give teachers the safety they need to struggle, we start to feel it long before we can fully name it. It shows up in the questions running through our heads:

Why do I have to follow up on everything?
Why does everyone wait to be told what to do?

We start to feel something change in the culture. Classroom visits feel tense. When we walk into a classroom with a clipboard, people panic. It feels like teachers are putting on a show instead of letting anyone see real instruction. The lesson may look smooth, and the routines may appear polished. Underneath it, something important is missing: risk-taking, experimentation, and honest conversations about what isn't working.

We see it in small moments all across our campuses.

A coach walks into a classroom where a teacher is clearly struggling and asks, "Do you want to work on this together?"

The teacher smiles and says, "No, I'm good."

Asking for help feels like admitting they're not capable, even when support is needed. When the line between learning and performance is unclear, struggle stops feeling like part of learning and starts feeling like evidence of failure. Practice happens safely behind closed doors instead of openly with colleagues.

Perfectionism starts running the building, and feedback gets harder as teachers shut down or become defensive during growth conversations. From the outside, it can begin to look like teachers are unwilling to grow, and that perception shapes how leaders respond.

Frustration starts to creep in.

Most teachers are working incredibly hard in an environment where performance feels constantly visible and mistakes feel costly. Over time, the energy in the building becomes more about protecting a sense of competence and away from developing it.

When Growth Mindset goes unsupported, schools lose safety.

The Shift

So how do we start to build a Growth Mindset culture in our schools?

Stop treating every moment like performance. When teachers feel constantly evaluated, they protect what they already know and hesitate to experiment with something new.

Start making the learning space visible by being explicit about when teachers are practicing versus being evaluated, protecting time for trial and error, and adjusting your support based on what they need in that moment.

When leaders learn to read the signals of effort and struggle, they stop pushing harder and start supporting smarter. Improvement happens because learning becomes possible.

The Core Idea

Make it safe to struggle.

The Practice

The Resistance Signal

In real time, a lack of Growth Mindset has a sound to it. You hear it in small, almost casual comments:

- "What I'm doing is working well enough."
- "I don't want to make things worse."
- "This feels really risky with these kids."
- "Can I just tweak what I already do instead?"
- "I'm afraid of doing it wrong."

Those moments are easy to move past, especially since they don't always come with intensity. Sometimes it's just a shrug or a quick comment before the conversation moves on. If you've been coaching or leading for a while, you can feel the pull to jump in to offer a strategy or model something new to help move things forward.

That instinct comes from a good place. Still, I've noticed that when I respond too quickly, I'm often solving for the wrong thing. What I'm hearing in those moments isn't really about strategy. It's someone trying to hold onto a sense of competence while stepping into something uncertain.

So I've learned to slow down just enough to stay with it. I listen a little longer and get curious about what might be underneath. Sometimes it's protection of something that already works. Sometimes It's the weight of the change. Sometimes there's a doubt about whether success is even possible.

I don't always know right away, but I've found that this moment matters. When I move too quickly into fixing, the pressure in the conversation rises, even if that's not my intention. And when that pressure rises, people tend to tense up. They say less and take fewer risks. When I stay with the curiosity a little longer, the conversation opens, and the support has somewhere to land.

The Tool: Effort–Struggle Matrix

Effort-Struggle Matrix

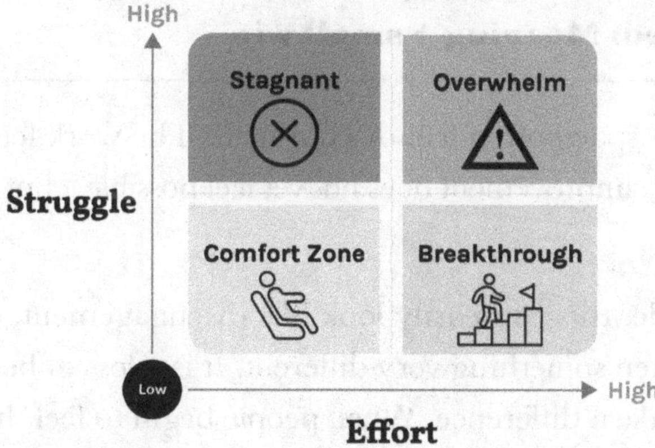

When someone is learning something new, two signals reveal what they need next:

Effort is a **motivation signal**.

Struggle is a **learning signal**.

The **Effort-Struggle Matrix** reveals two primary leadership responses.

When struggle is high → create small wins.

Break the work into tiny steps, guide experimentation, and make progress visible.

When effort is low → reconnect meaning and achievability.

Link the change to something the teacher values, and help them see that progress is possible.

The Four Quadrants

Stagnation Zone

> Low Effort + High Struggle
> **Primary need: Meaning + small win**

Teachers in this space often feel discouraged. The work feels difficult, and because improvement does not yet feel possible, effort begins to fade.

From the outside, this can easily look like disengagement, but underneath it is often something very different. It is a loss of belief that progress will make a difference. When people begin to feel that their effort will not change the outcome, motivation naturally drops.

The leadership goal in this zone is twofold:

1. Reconnect the work to something meaningful.
2. Then create a small, visible success that restores belief.

Meaning helps teachers care about the work again. Small wins help them see that improvement is possible.

When teachers experience even a small amount of progress, effort often begins to return.

Concrete Coaching Strategies

1. **Rebuild relevance before rigor.** Ask, "What part of this work feels meaningful to you right now?" or "Which part of this goal connects most to what you care about?"
2. **Design one visible success.** Work together to set a "tiny tweak" goal to ensure they experience an early win that restores confidence.
3. **Chunk and choose.** Break big initiatives into smaller, teacher-selected goals to increase ownership and reduce overwhelm.

Overwhelm Zone

High Effort + High Struggle
Primary need: Small win

Teachers in this zone are trying hard, but nothing seems to click yet.

They are experimenting, adjusting, and investing significant energy without seeing results. This is where frustration can build quickly. When effort stays high but progress remains unclear, discouragement often begins to creep in. Without support, the energy teachers are investing can turn into burnout.

Teachers in this zone need help experiencing a small success. They need **partnership**.

Breaking the work into manageable pieces can make an immediate difference. Co-planning one lesson together, modeling a single strategy, or focusing on one adjustment instead of many can help reduce the complexity of the task.

Once teachers see a strategy working, belief begins to rebuild and learning becomes more sustainable.

Concrete Coaching Strategies

1. **Share the load.** Use "we" language: "Let's tackle this part together," or "We can try this one change and see how it goes," or "I see how hard you're working at this. Let's look at what might make it easier."
2. **Reduce variables.** Help educators focus on one key area of improvement instead of chasing multiple changes at once.
3. **Co-plan and co-teach.** Plan the next lesson together, so the teacher doesn't have to figure everything out alone and facilitate it together.

Comfort Zone

Low Effort + Low Struggle
Primary need: Meaningful stretch

In this zone, things are working well enough.

Lessons run smoothly, students are generally engaged, and classroom routines feel predictable. From the outside the classroom may appear stable and successful, but but not much growth is actually happening. Teachers in the comfort zone often avoid experimentation as they work to protect what is already working.

The leadership goal here centers on meaning.

Growth begins when a challenge connects to something the teacher genuinely cares about: a student need, classroom goal, or problem they want to solve.

When the work feels personally meaningful, effort begins to rise naturally.

Concrete Coaching Strategies

1. **Start with affirmation.** Recognize their successes genuinely: "Your classroom runs so smoothly. It's clear you have strong systems in place."
2. **Co-create a stretch goal.** Ask, "If you could improve one thing for your students, what would it be?" Identify one meaningful area to refine or innovate that connects to something they value.
3. **Invite peer observation.** After a meaningful goal is set, pair them with another teacher experimenting successfully in a related area to normalize growth as a collective pursuit.

Breakthrough Zone

High Effort + Low Struggle
Primary need: Extend growth and reinforce learning

This is where productive learning is happening.

Teachers are investing strong effort and beginning to see results. The struggle has become manageable and productive. Belief in improvement is strengthening and teachers begin recognizing that their actions influence outcomes.

The leadership move here is to reinforce and extend the learning. Celebrate the progress, reflect on what worked, and invite teachers to share their learning with colleagues.

Breakthrough moments matter because they build confidence, strengthen belief, and encourage continued experimentation.

Concrete Coaching Strategies

1. **Celebrate effort and growth.** Publicly acknowledge their effort and learning, not just outcomes, to model a growth culture.
2. **Reflect on agency.** Ask, "What did you do that helped this work so well?" or "What changes did you make that you're proud of?"
3. **Invite mentorship.** Encourage them to share what's working with peers, reinforcing their confidence and spreading effective practice.

Effort–Struggle Matrix Summary

The Effort–Struggle Matrix focuses on noticing signals. Effort tells you whether the work feels meaningful enough to invest in. Struggle tells you where someone currently sits in the learning process. When leaders misread these signals, they often coach the wrong thing. The Effort–Struggle Matrix helps leaders slow down, notice the signals, and respond to what teachers actually need. Leaders can move away from pushing harder, rescuing too quickly, or assuming resistance and ask a better question:

What does this person need in order to keep learning?

The Effort-Struggle Matrix Tool In Action

Scenario

Here are some examples of how this could look:

Mr. Carter

Mr. Carter reuses the same essay prompts every year. When colleagues suggest updating the assignment, he shrugs and says, "Kids these days just don't try." Student writing remains weak, but he rarely changes the task.

Stagnation Zone: Low Effort + High Struggle

Common misread: He's lazy, stuck in his ways, and doesn't want to change.

Actual signal: The work feels difficult and improvement doesn't feel achievable. Instead of experimenting with his own practice, he defaults to familiar routines and attributes the problem to students.

When effort is low and struggle is high, it often means belief has dropped. He doesn't yet see how his actions could meaningfully improve the outcome.

Coaching move: Start small and stack wins. Help him revise just one prompt for an upcoming lesson and notice what changes. The goal is to create a small, visible success that rebuilds belief and gets him moving again.

Mr. Johnson

Mr. Johnson stays up late tweaking lessons and calling parents, but his class still feels chaotic.

Overwhelm Zone: High Effort + High Struggle

Common misread: He needs better management, more structure, or to stop overthinking everything.

Actual diagnosis: He's putting in significant effort, but the constant struggle and cognitive load are keeping him from stabilizing any one practice. He's fully in the work, and it's overwhelming him.

Coaching move: Create a small win. Partner up and pare down. Co-plan one routine together, model it if possible, and remove competing priorities so he can experience success in one manageable area before adding anything new.

Ms. Lopez

Ms. Lopez's lessons run smoothly and her students behave. But when asked to try student-led discussions, she smiles and says, "My kids just aren't ready." Everything works, but nothing grows.

Comfort Zone: Low Effort + Low Struggle

Common misread: Her class is running well. This isn't the thing to push right now.

Actual diagnosis: Her practice is stable and effective, but it isn't being stretched. Low struggle signals she's operating in familiar territory where growth isn't being activated.

Coaching move: Introduce a meaningful stretch that matters to her. Identify one place she already cares about improving student thinking and layer in student voice there, such as a short partner discussion or student-generated questions. The goal is to stretch the practice without disrupting what's already working.

Ms. Nguyen

Ms. Nguyen has been working on the new strategy for a few weeks. Her routines are tighter, transitions are smoother, and students are beginning to take more ownership during the lesson. It's not perfect, but there's clear traction. She's putting in strong effort, and the struggle is now productive rather than overwhelming.

Breakthrough Zone: High Effort + Low Struggle

Common misread: She's got it now. Time to move on.

Actual diagnosis: Effort is still high, and the struggle moves from survival to refinement. This is the moment where growth is accelerating, not finished.

Coaching move: Extend the learning. Help her analyze what's working, refine one higher-level move, and apply the strategy in a new context so the learning deepens instead of plateauing.

What Just Happened

Each teacher needed a safer place to learn.

Until that moment, the focus had been on improving performance. The real barrier sat in the environment around the learning. Once the leader clarified the learning space and supported one manageable step, the teacher could stay in the process long enough for improvement to begin.

The change happened as the experience of learning became manageable.

The Coaching Shift

When teachers struggle, it's easy to respond by adding more. More feedback, more expectations, more strategies. It feels responsible in the moment. Still, when someone already feels exposed in their learning, that added pressure can slow things down instead of moving them forward.

A better place to start is with a simple pause. Ask yourself, "Where are they in the learning process right now?" That question has a way of changing everything. It pulls you out of reacting and into noticing.

From there, the response becomes more grounded. When effort is low, the work often needs to reconnect to meaning and feel within reach. When struggle is high, what helps most is a small, manageable step that lets the person stay in it a little longer.

As the learning signal becomes clearer, the support starts to take shape. You're no longer guessing or pushing. You're responding to what's actually happening in front of you.

Use It Tomorrow

Listen for the learning signals:

* "What I'm doing is working well enough."
* "I don't want to make things worse."
* "I'm afraid of doing it wrong."

Don't jump straight to correction. Start here:

* Notice the effort signal.
* Notice the struggle signal.

Then match the support:

* Reconnect the work to meaning.
* Or create a small win.

Stay in the learning zone long enough for progress to appear because that's where the Growth Mindset actually develops.

Summary

At its core, the Growth Mindset is the belief that ability can improve through effort, learning, and feedback. But that belief does not grow from slogans or encouragement alone. It develops through support, strategies, and experience.

When educators have space to practice, struggle, and refine their work without fear of judgment, learning begins to accelerate. But when the line between learning and performance becomes unclear, the experience of learning changes. Struggle starts to feel risky, mistakes begin to feel like proof of incompetence, and teachers start putting their energy into protecting their practice instead of developing it.

Leaders play a critical role in shaping these conditions. By paying attention to the signals of effort and struggle, leaders can better understand the experience teachers are having as they try something new. The Effort–Struggle Matrix helps make those signals visible.

When effort is low, reconnect the work to meaning and achievability. When struggle is high, create small wins that stabilize learning.

Growth happens when the conditions make it possible.

Reflection Questions

1. Think about a teacher you are currently supporting. Based on what you are observing, which Effort–Struggle zone might they be operating in right now?
2. What signals are you noticing? What evidence do you see of their level of effort and the level of struggle they may be experiencing?
3. What is one leadership move you could make this week that would better match the support to their zone?

Bonus Resources

The **Growth Mindset Response Tool** includes coaching stems for each quadrant to help guide conversations that support growth.

Access this and other bonus resources at **thewholeeducator.com/book-resources**.

Chapter 8:
Ownership Mindset

"They Won't Show Up to PLCs"

"They won't show up to PLCs," Ms. T, a second-year instructional coach, sighed for the third week in a row. Every visit, the story was the same. She'd crafted flawless reminder emails, color-coded calendars, even offered snacks, but her teachers kept ghosting her. Lesson plans trickled in late and the hallway shuffle was real. She'd turn the corner and watch teachers spot her, then immediately pivot and disappear into classrooms.

Ms. T was skilled and committed, and she was exhausted. She'd tried everything that should work, and still, her team was avoiding her like she carried a clipboard of bad news. By the time she joined my Academy, she was burned out, irritated, and tired of being ignored. In group coaching, she'd vent about her teachers, how they didn't care, how they wouldn't step up. And beneath the frustration, what I really heard was disappointment. She cared deeply, but the more she chased compliance, the more disconnected she felt.

Then one session, she hit a turning point. During our Ownership exercise, she confronted her own limiting belief, the one that said her teachers were lazy. That belief had quietly kept her on defense, patching relationships together with reminder emails, accountability checklists, and relentless positivity. When she replaced that belief with a new one, that her teachers had unmet needs and she needed to find out what they were, everything changed.

She started asking teachers what they needed and how they were feeling about their classrooms. She stopped defending and started listening, really listening, with curiosity and compassion. For the first time, those answers weren't rushed past or explained away, and that's when things started to change.

Within weeks, teachers started showing up at her office asking for help because they wanted support. They shared ideas, talked through challenges, and began taking more initiative in their classrooms. What had felt like compliance started to feel like ownership, and the collaborative culture she'd been hoping for began to form.

Progress begins when ownership replaces blame.

The Mindset: Ownership

When the coach replaced her "lazy teachers" belief with an Ownership Mindset, everything began to change. The change came through how she showed up as a leader, not because the teachers suddenly became different people. The quiet power of ownership changes how we see others, which changes how we show up for them. The difference came through a change in mindset.

The belief underneath the Ownership Mindset is simple:

I believe I can change things by taking responsibility.

What matters here is that the coach's first story wasn't unusual and didn't come out of nowhere. It was learned over time within a system that has normalized a Compliance Culture as the default way we "do school," which is one of the biggest reasons the Ownership Mindset so often goes unsupported.

The thing to understand is that ownership develops through cultivation over time, not through enforcement, and the research consistently points to five elements that need to be supported for it to take hold.

- Value Mindset
- Belonging Mindset
- Success Mindset
- Growth Mindset
- Agency

We have discussed the four mindsets in previous chapters, but agency is the fifth required element for ownership. Agency is *the ability and opportunity to make intentional choices and take meaningful action*. Internal agency is the belief that your actions can make a difference. External agency is whether the environment actually gives you the autonomy, support, and trust to act on that belief.

When any one of these elements is unsupported, ownership collapses into lower Levels of Engagement (see Chapter 1). When they align, people stop waiting to be told what to do and start taking initiative. The way educators show up in their work often reflects which of these beliefs are currently supported.

When these conditions aren't present, schools often develop patterns that quietly undermine ownership.

Why Leaders Struggle to Support This Mindset

We genuinely want teachers to take initiative, think creatively, and feel responsible for the success of their students, but many of the leadership practices we've learned actually steer us towards compliance.

One main way we do this is by focusing too much on building buy-in. In many leadership programs, buy-in is presented as the goal. We explain the vision, address concerns, and help people get on board. When teachers agree or say the plan makes sense, we assume the work is moving forward. As discussed in Chapter 1, buy-in and ownership are not the same thing. Buy-in means people agree with the plan. Ownership means people feel responsible for the outcome.

Buy-in asks, "Do you support this?"

Ownership asks, "How will you help shape this?"

For example, a school has decided to increase student discourse during classroom discussions. In a buy-in approach, teachers are shown one strategy during professional learning and expected to implement it in their classrooms. Teachers may (or may not) agree the strategy makes sense and try it as presented.

In an ownership approach, the goal stays the same, but the path is more open. Teachers might be introduced to several strategies that support student talk time and invited to choose the one that fits their classroom or develop their own approach based on what they know about their students.

When we focus primarily on gaining buy-in, teachers may support the initiative and follow expectations, but they are still carrying out someone else's thinking. Ownership grows when educators influence the work itself, deciding how it fits their students and their context. Another challenge is that most of us were trained inside compliance cultures. Schools have long assumed that clear expectations and strong accountability will lead to responsibility. When we don't see progress, our instinct is to clarify the plan, tighten the structure, or reinforce the expectation.

Those moves can increase action in the short term, but they also send a quiet message: the thinking has already been done. When the thinking has already been done, people learn to wait.

In many schools, educators have learned that using their professional judgment can get them in trouble, so compliance feels safer than initiative. When teachers hesitate, leaders often interpret it as attitude and miss the signal that agency hasn't been built yet.

Ownership develops differently. It grows when educators believe their actions matter and have the opportunity to shape the work itself.

The Silent Progress Blocker: Leader-Dependent Culture

Each year, school leaders set goals for improvement. Leaders review data, identify priorities, and work with an instructional leadership team to determine what the school should focus on. A plan is developed, strategies are chosen, and benchmarks are set. Then the plan is shared with the staff. Teachers hear the goals, the strategies, and the expectations for implementation. The direction is clear, and the work begins, but another barrier quietly shows up here.

Leaders often assume teachers know where they are expected to use their professional judgment and where the work is non-negotiable. In reality, those boundaries are rarely made explicit. Some teachers hesitate because past experiences taught them that using their judgment can get them in trouble. Others hesitate because they've learned to wait for permission before acting. When the space for professional judgment isn't clearly defined, people default to compliance.

Something subtle also happens in this process. The thinking has already been done. Teachers may support the goals and agree the priorities make sense, but the work still belongs to the people who designed the plan. Teachers are responsible for implementing it.

For example, a leadership team may set a schoolwide goal to strengthen student writing across content areas. In a leader-dependent approach, the leadership team also decides how the school will accomplish that goal. They select the strategies, determine the plan, and then present it to staff for implementation. Over time, a leader-dependent culture begins to form. This causes teachers to wait for direction and grade-level meetings focus on carrying out the plan. Consequently, leadership teams drive the thinking while everyone else follows the path that was set. Responsibility for the work was never distributed in the first place.

Ownership grows when people have the opportunity to influence the work itself. When educators help define the problems, shape the strategies, and test solutions in their classrooms, the work becomes something they feel responsible for. Ownership is supported when leaders clearly name two things: what must stay consistent and where educators are expected to use their professional judgment.

In a system that supports ownership, the goal might still be set by leadership, and the conversation about how to reach it happens with the staff. Teachers help explore the problem, suggest strategies, test ideas in their classrooms, and share what works. The goal is shared, and the thinking is distributed. Without that change, the system unintentionally trains people to wait, which keeps ownership from ever fully taking root.

The Cost of Getting This Wrong

When ownership is weak, leaders and coaches feel it immediately. The work gets heavier and momentum depends on constant reminders. Progress only happens when someone is watching. Leaders feel like they're dragging change forward alone. They re-explain expectations, chase follow-through, and hold the emotional weight of improvement while others stay in passive roles. The moment oversight disappears, initiatives start to fall apart, and it begins to feel like if they stop pushing, everything will stop.

Coaches feel it just as sharply. They become project managers instead of developers of people. They make the plans, send reminders, and keep the work moving while teachers follow along. Coaching cycles start strong but lose momentum quickly. Conversations circle the same problems. Teachers ask for advice but don't act on it. Progress happens when the coach is present and fades when they step away. It begins to feel like they're working harder than the person they're coaching.

Teams feel it too. Instead of taking initiative, people begin waiting for permission before acting. Teachers arrive at meetings unprepared and rely on others to carry the thinking forward. PLCs slowly become something people avoid rather than a space they actively contribute to, much like the team Ms. T described at the beginning of this chapter. Problem-solving conversations drift into venting, and good ideas almost never translate into action. Teachers follow through on what is monitored while letting everything else fade away. Collaboration loses its generative energy, and innovation ends up depending on a small group of self-starters while everyone else falls into step behind them.

Over time, the emotional toll builds and leaders feel exhausted from driving the momentum alone. Frustration turns into quiet resentment and doubt creeps in about whether change is actually possible. It starts to feel like people say they want improvement but won't take responsibility for making it happen.

What becomes most damaging over time is how the work starts to rely on pressure instead of purpose. Initiative disappears and leaders and coaches are left doing the heavy lifting of change that was never meant to be theirs alone.

The Shift

So how do we start to build ownership in our schools?

Stop carrying the thinking, the planning, and the momentum of the work. When leaders hold all the responsibility, initiative fades and people begin to wait for direction. Conversations turn to, "Just tell me what you want," and improvement depends on constant reminders and oversight.

Start facilitating conditions where educators help to shape the work. Ownership grows when people have the opportunity to influence the problems being solved, the strategies being tested, and the path forward for their students. Responsibility spreads as people see that their thinking matters and their actions move the work. Progress comes from shared responsibility.

The Core Idea

Let educators shape the work, not just implement it.

The Practice

The Resistance Signal

In the moment, this form of resistance has a familiar sound. You might hear teachers say:

- "Just tell me what you want me to do."
- "That decision's already been made."
- "There's nothing I can do"
- "It is what it is."
- "I'm just doing what I'm told."

When you hear language like this, it is important to pause rather than react. The instinct in these moments is often to push harder, clarify expectations again, or hold people more tightly to the plan. Most of us have been trained to do exactly that. This is usually an ownership problem.

The coaching cue is simple, but not always easy: slow down and re-build a sense of agency. Before offering direction, consider where they feel shut down, what feels out of their hands, and where there might be room for choice or influence. Moving too quickly to control can deepen disengagement. Staying in curiosity helps them begin to see where they can have impact again. Agency opens the door to own-ership, but people still need a way to step through it. So the question becomes: *How do we help someone step into that responsibility?*

One way is to give people a simple structure for turning concern into action. The **G.R.I.P. Framework** helps leaders and coaches do ex-actly that. It creates a conversation where educators begin identifying the next step they're willing to take.

The Tool: G.R.I.P. Framework

Leaders often ask, "How do I help someone move from compliance to ownership?"

Ownership grows when educators move from reacting to problems to designing their next step forward. The **G.R.I.P. Framework** gives leaders and coaches a simple structure to make that happen..

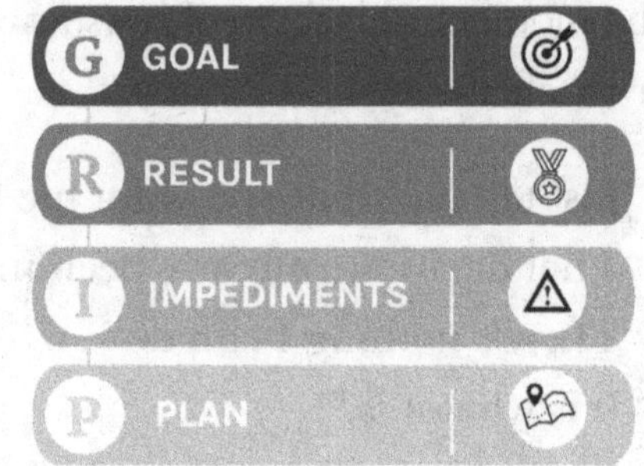

G.R.I.P. stands for **Goal, Result, Impediments, Plan**. It helps educators clarify what they want, anticipate obstacles, and take intentional action.

Each step of G.R.I.P. strengthens a different part of the Ownership Mindset.

- **Goal** builds Value and direction.
- **Result** strengthens belief in Success.
- **Impediments** activate Growth by anticipating challenges.
- **Plan** turns Agency into action.

As people walk through G.R.I.P., they begin to see where they can shape the work instead of just responding to it. Ownership moves from idea to action.

Using G.R.I.P. in a Coaching Conversation

Imagine you are working with a teacher stuck in **Compliance** on the Levels of Engagement continuum. The teacher is doing what's required but without energy or belief. The coach begins with G.R.I.P.:

- **Goal:** "What do you want your students to walk away knowing by the end of this unit?"
- **Result:** "If everything went perfectly, what would it look or sound like in your classroom?"
- **Impediments:** "What might get in the way of that vision?"
- **Plan:** "What's one change you're willing to try this week, and how can I support you in it?"

By the end of the conversation, the teacher has moved from *following a plan* to *creating one*, which is where ownership starts to grow.

G.R.I.P. Step-by-Step Breakdown

Let's walk through each part of G.R.I.P. and why it matters.

Goal

The Goal sets the direction of improvement. It answers a simple question: *What do I want to accomplish?* It's about naming something real, energizing, and **relevant**. Ownership starts when people name how *they* want to grow, not something we've already defined for them.

> We're not saying, "I want to get better at classroom management." We're saying, "I want students to transition between activities smoothly and stay engaged for the full lesson."

Ask yourself the following:

1. What do I want to achieve?
2. How is it relevant, meaningful, or purposeful to me?
3. Why does this matter right now?

Setting a clear goal supports the **Value Mindset** because it connects the work to what matters to the person setting it.

Warning: If the coach sets the goal instead of co-creating it with the teacher, it will not support the Value Mindset and ownership will weaken. A crucial part of this process is that the teacher must be genuinely invested in the goal. When the goal matters to them, it activates relevance, meaning, and purpose. (See the Value Mindset chapter for more guidance on this.)

Tip: Don't perfect the goal, just name the direction. You'll define what success looks like in the next step.

Result

The Result makes the goal concrete. It gives the direction a clear, visible target.

A result is **specific, measurable, and observable**. It answers a simple question: **How will I know when I've achieved it?**

> Example:
> **Goal:** "I want students to transition between activities smoothly and stay engaged for the full lesson."
> **Result:** "Students begin transitions within 15 seconds of a cue, and 90 percent are on task within one minute."

When goals move from general to measurable, the intention becomes visible in real ways, and that's where the Success Mindset starts to strengthen. When educators can clearly see what success looks like, belief grows that it is possible, and as success becomes visible, motivation and accountability grow naturally.

Take it one step further. Make the result easy to picture. What would you see students or staff doing? What would it sound like? What would feel different?

If you can see it clearly, it becomes easier to move toward it.

Impediments

This step is, in my opinion, the most powerful step. Naming impediments is strategic. Highly effective leaders anticipate obstacles before they derail progress.

This step strengthens the **Growth Mindset** by helping educators expect challenges instead of being surprised by them. People with a Growth Mindset don't avoid difficulty. They prepare for it and persist through it.

Ask yourself the following questions:

1. What **internal** beliefs or fears might hold me back?
2. What **external** systems or conditions could get in the way?
3. Which of these are within my **influence**, and which are not?

Impediments usually include a mix of both.

Internal impediments may include the following:

- Self-doubt or perfectionism that makes risk-taking feel harder
- Frustration from past failed attempts
- A belief that "nothing will change here anyway"
- Fear of judgment or loss of control

External impediments may include the following:

- Limited time or competing initiatives
- Unclear leadership expectations
- Lack of collaboration or follow-through from colleagues
- Inconsistent administrative support
- Structural barriers such as scheduling, resources, or policy restrictions

Modeling how to anticipate multiple impediments helps normalize challenges as part of the process rather than proof of inadequacy.

> For example: A teacher wants to improve student engagement during discussions. They identify three likely impediments: time pressure to cover content (external), discomfort with silence (internal), and inconsistent student participation (external).

By naming these obstacles in advance, the teacher can plan supports such as reducing the number of discussion questions, practicing intentional wait time, and assigning discussion roles. When we learn to predict our own barriers, we reclaim our power.

Awareness turns frustration into foresight and strengthens agency. When obstacles are visible, people can decide how to respond instead of feeling stuck by them.

The goal is to make impediments visible enough that they no longer control the outcome.

Plan

This is where ownership becomes visible. The Plan turns insight into intentional action by focusing on a realistic step forward and staying responsive when things get messy. It also brings a level of intentionality to the process by planning ahead for likely impediments. What will we do when they show up? Even better, how might we proactively avoid them?

Ask yourself the following questions:

1. What specific step will move me closer to my result?
2. What support or accountability will help me follow through?
3. How will I adjust if obstacles arise?

For making the Plan, I like to use these sentence frames:

If [impediment] happens, then I will [intentional action].
To avoid [impediment], I will [intentional action].

Below are several examples:

- **If** I run short on time, **then** I will focus on one key strategy (instead of trying to implement everything at once).
- **If** students do not respond immediately, **then** I will use a structured pair-share strategy (instead of abandoning the plan).
- **To** stay encouraged, **I will** share small wins each week with a trusted colleague.

> - **To** avoid slipping back into old habits, **I will** post my goal where I can see it and review it before each lesson.
> - **When** external factors are outside my control, **I will** focus my energy on the elements of practice that are within my influence.

The Plan step integrates all five elements of the Ownership Mindset:

Value: actions connect to what matters most.

Success: progress becomes achievable and visible.

Belonging: collaboration and feedback strengthen commitment.

Growth: obstacles become opportunities to adapt and learn.

Agency: control returns to the educator's hands.

A plan, even a small one, gives people a place to begin.

The G.R.I.P. Framework Tool In Action

Scenario

A literacy coach I worked with once described herself as a "professional remind-er." Every week she sent the same emails: Don't forget your lesson plans. Please update your small-group schedule. Remember to turn in your data. She was organized, dedicated, and exhausted. Her teachers weren't showing up prepared for meetings, and many seemed disengaged.

One afternoon, she decided to try G.R.I.P. with a teacher who had been stuck in compliance. Instead of sending another reminder, she invited a conversation.

Goal

"What do you want your students to take away from small-group reading this month?"

The teacher hesitated. "Honestly, I just want them to stop zoning out during guided reading."

The coach didn't move past that. She stayed with it and helped the teacher shape it into something that actually mattered to her, not just something that sounded right.

"What would feel different for you if that changed?"

The teacher paused. "I wouldn't feel like I'm dragging them through the lesson," she said. "I'd actually feel like they're with me."

That change mattered because the goal wasn't just about fixing student behavior. It was about creating a classroom experience that felt more engaging and more manageable for her.

They named the goal simply: students actively participating in small-group reading.

Result

"If that happened, if they were really engaged, what would that look like?"

"They'd be talking about the book instead of staring at me," she said, her tone shifting as the idea started to click.

They pushed a little further.

"What would you actually see or hear?"

"More students responding… building off each other… not just waiting for me."

Now the goal had a clear picture behind it, so the teacher could actually see what it would look like in practice, and that gave them something specific to aim for.

Impediments

Then they paused and named what might get in the way.

"Okay… what could make this hard or not successful?"

The teacher didn't hesitate this time. "They struggle to focus." **[students disengaging]** "Students don't know how to respond to each other." **[struggle to respond]** "And honestly, I feel rushed trying to get through everything." **[time pressure]**

Saying them out loud made the challenges clear and specific, instead of leaving them in the background where they quietly shaped what happened. Once they were visible, they became something the teacher could actually address and work through.

Plan

Instead of jumping to a big solution, they kept it small and specific.

"What's one thing you'd be willing to try this week?"

They landed on one discussion move: **a simple partner-talk structure before whole-group sharing**.

Then they made a plan to address the impediments:

* "If **time pressure** shows up, then I will focus on one key discussion question instead of trying to cover everything."

- "To avoid **students disengaging**, I will assign clear partner roles so everyone has a job during the discussion."
- "If students **struggle to respond**, then I will model one strong response before asking them to try."

The intentional plan gave the teacher something she could actually do, and a way to stay with it when things didn't go perfectly the first time.

The next day, when the coach returned, the teacher was waiting at her door.

"It worked," she said, smiling. "The students actually talked about the book. I think I just needed to try something different."

Something important had shifted, as the teacher moved beyond simply completing a requirement and began designing her own solution. At the same time, the coach stepped out of managing compliance and into a role that supported real ownership. The G.R.I.P. process changed who was carrying the work, with the thinking no longer driven by the coach but owned by the teacher. This is where ownership starts to take root, as people begin to see that their actions can shape the outcome. Over time, that belief gives way to initiative, replacing checklists and reminders.

Use It Tomorrow

Pay attention to the language that signals a loss of ownership:

- "Just tell me what you want me to do."
- "That decision's already been made."
- "There's nothing I can do here."
- "I'm just doing what I'm told."

Resist the urge to tighten control or restate expectations.

Try this instead:

- Explore where they feel stuck or shut down.
- Surface what feels out of their control.
- Look for one place where they still have influence.
- Stay in that space long enough for them to see a next step they're willing to take.

People start taking ownership here. Once they can see a next step, you can help them turn it into a clear plan.

Summary

At its core, the Ownership Mindset is the belief that *I can influence what happens here by taking responsibility*. Ownership grows when people believe their actions matter and when the environment gives them the space to act on that belief. This chapter showed how easily schools fall into leader-dependent patterns. Leaders carry the thinking, teachers implement the plan, and initiative slowly disappears. Over time, people learn to wait for direction instead of shaping solutions themselves.

Ownership grows when educators see the value of the work, feel a sense of belonging in the environment, believe they can succeed, and trust they can grow through challenge. When those beliefs are supported and educators have real agency to influence the work, responsibility begins to grow. Instead of implementing someone else's plan, educators begin shaping the work themselves. Initiative replaces reminders and accountability becomes something people embrace rather than something leaders enforce.

Ownership is something leaders cultivate by sharing the thinking, expanding agency, and supporting educators to lead their own growth.

Reflection Questions

1. How clearly have I communicated the nonnegotiables versus where teachers are encouraged and expected to use their professional judgment?
2. Where do teachers currently have real voice and choice in how the work happens, and where am I unintentionally over-structuring or holding the wheel?
3. How will I use G.R.I.P. to support teachers in developing ownership instead of stepping in to carry the work?

Bonus Resources

The **Agency Audit** helps leaders assess the conditions that either support or limit teacher agency so they can create environments where ownership is more likely to grow.

Access this and other bonus resources at **thewholeeducator.com/book-resources**.

Chapter 9

Human-Centered Accountability

When Support Isn't Enough

At its core, accountability creates structure around the work. It brings focus to what matters most, makes progress visible, and helps people see how their effort connects to something real. It gives the work a shared direction so it doesn't rely on interpretation or good intentions alone. The reality is not all accountability works the same way.

In many schools, accountability quietly turns into what I would call **compliance-based accountability**, driven by a well-intentioned desire to ensure the work happens consistently and produces results.

The difference shows up in how we respond in the moment.

Compliance-Based Accountability

- "I'd like to see more engagement in your lesson."
- "Let's make sure you're implementing the strategy consistently."
- "I'll come back next week to check on this."

The focus stays on **what needs to happen.**

The assumption is: *they should already be able to do this.*

Human-Centered Accountability

- "I'd like to see more engagement in your lesson. What's been getting in the way?"
- "Walk me through what you've tried so far."
- "Where does this feel unclear or hard right now?"

The focus moves to **what's making it hard.**

The assumption is: *something underneath may need support.*

The moves can look similar on the surface, with a check-in, a follow-up, or a clearly stated expectation, but what ultimately matters is what unfolds after those moments.

In compliance-based accountability, we stay at the level of behavior. When it's not happening, we restate expectations or increase follow-through. Over time, that will start to feel like pressure.

In human-centered accountability, we still hold the expectation, but we pay attention to something different. Instead of stopping at what's visible, we start understanding what's underneath it. We look for the belief, the barrier, or the unmet need shaping what we're seeing, and we respond to that. That change alters the experience of the work.

People still know what they're working toward, and progress is still visible, but now they also feel supported in getting there. Conversations build instead of restarting, feedback becomes more specific, and effort starts to stack instead of scatter.

The work becomes more shared. Direction stays consistent, commitments are easier to follow through on, and people can see where they fit and how their actions contribute.

It stops feeling abstract and starts to feel real.

Mindsets shape how people think and engage. Accountability is what carries that thinking into the work itself. It creates the conditions for those beliefs to show up in consistent, intentional action.

Support or Accountability?

Most of this book has pushed against one extreme: compliance-driven accountability. The kind that relies on pressure, monitoring, and "just do it" leadership. It creates motion, sometimes quickly, but it rarely creates commitment, and over time, it wears people down. So it makes sense that leaders have moved away from it. But in some of the schools where I work, I see a different extreme. Leaders lean hard into support and create cultures that feel good but lack structure, direction, and shared purpose. When we overcorrect in either direction, we don't get the best of both and the work gets diluted.

When accountability is overdone, it stops being about the work and starts being about control. Expectations get enforced without being understood, follow-through gets monitored without being supported, and people start protecting themselves instead of engaging. You might see compliance on the surface, but underneath, people are calculating risk, avoiding mistakes, and doing just enough to stay out of trouble. The work moves, but it doesn't deepen. It becomes performative instead of meaningful. Over time, that kind of pressure chips away at ownership because when people don't feel safe to think, question, or try, they stop investing. Accountability without support doesn't build commitment. It builds quiet resistance.

When support is overdone, the opposite problem shows up. The culture feels good, conversations are thoughtful, and people feel seen, but the work starts to drift. Without clear expectations and shared definitions of success, everyone interprets the goal a little differently. People leave conversations feeling encouraged, but not always sure what they're actually responsible for doing next. Follow-through becomes optional because nothing is anchoring the work in something concrete. Over time, progress becomes inconsistent, then hard to see at all. Support without accountability doesn't move the work forward. It keeps people comfortable while things stay the same.

Redefining Accountability

Accountability has a reputation problem.

Most of us hear that word and think about pressure, compliance, getting called out or someone checking to see if something got done. It feels external, weighty, and like something people try to avoid or work around, no matter which side of it they're on. That's not what we're talking about here.

At its core, accountability is about high standards and challenging goals. It's the expectation that the work we are doing matters and that it is going somewhere meaningful.

Accountability is **knowing what good looks like and being expected to get there.**

What Human-Centered Accountability Does

At its core, accountability creates structure around the work. It brings focus to what matters most, makes progress visible, and helps people see how their effort connects to something real. It gives the work a shared direction so it doesn't rely on individual interpretation or good intentions alone. This is where the work starts to stick.

This is what changes when accountability is clear. People know what they're working toward, they can see what progress looks like and recognize when they're moving. Conversations build instead of re-starting, feedback becomes more specific and effort starts to stack instead of scatter.

At the same time, the work becomes more visible and more shared. Direction stays consistent, commitments are easier to follow through on, and people can see where they fit and how their actions contribute. It stops feeling abstract and starts to feel real.

Mindsets shape how people think and engage. Accountability is what carries that thinking into the work itself. It creates the conditions for those beliefs to show up in consistent, intentional action.

The Four Zones

Amy Edmondson's research on psychological safety showed that when people feel safe, they speak up, and that's where learning starts. As she continued her work, another insight emerged. Safety on its own didn't produce strong results. The teams that improved were the ones where people felt safe and were also held to high standards. That's what led to her

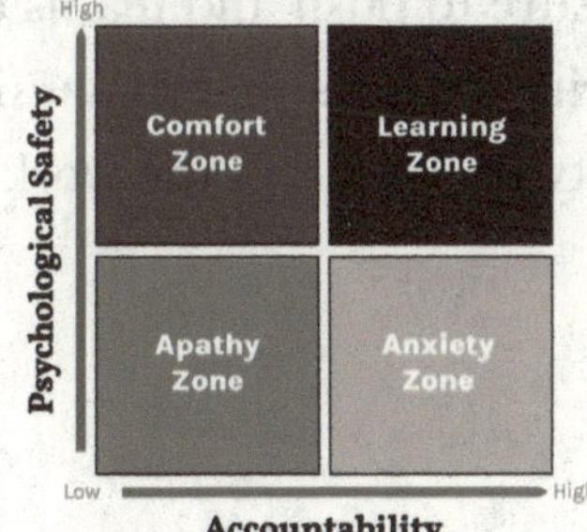

Taxonomy of Archetypal Zones

Adapted from Edmonson AC. Teaming: How Organizations Learn, Innovate, and Compete in the Knowledge Economy. John Wiley & Sons; 2012

Learning Zone, where psychological safety and accountability work together to drive both learning and performance.

- **Learning → high safety + high accountability**
- Comfort → high safety + low accountability
- Anxiety → low safety + high accountability
- Apathy → low safety + low accountability

Only one of these actually moves people forward.

The Accountability Check

A Work Clarity Diagnostic

When momentum slows, leaders often look first at people. A more useful starting point is the work itself. Before focusing on individuals, examine the structure around the work.

- ☐ Is the goal clear enough that everyone can name it and see their role?
- ☐ Is progress visible in a way that connects effort to movement?
- ☐ Are actions aligned with the goal?

When these are weak, accountability feels personal. Leaders feel pressure to push and teams experience expectations as inconsistent. Clarity changes that dynamic. It creates fairness and keeps accountability grounded in the work rather than personal judgment.

The Leadership Approach

Support meets unmet needs. Accountability protects the work. Those ideas can feel like they pull in different directions, especially in the middle of real conversations. In practice, leadership asks us to hold both at once. It asks us to stay deeply connected to people while also staying committed to the work that matters.

In those moments, it often comes down to three moves: acknowledge, ask, and anchor.

Acknowledge what you're seeing.
Ask what's getting in the way.
Anchor back to the expectation.

That "ask" is where you start to understand what's underneath the resistance. You're listening for which Catalyst Mindsets™ might be unsupported.

"I know you've been working on this. What's getting in the way right now? We still need to see students on task within a minute."

"I can see the effort you're putting in. What's feeling hardest about this? Let's figure out what's getting in the way here. We're going to stay with this until we see it working."

Support keeps people in the work. Accountability keeps the work moving.

When accountability is healthy, it doesn't disrupt the Catalyst Mindsets™. It gives them somewhere to thrive. It's what allows those beliefs to move out of conversation and into daily intentional action.

Conclusion

Leading Differently When Resistance Appears

Resistance shows up all the time when you're leading change. You see it when expectations shift, when the risk starts to feel real, when the path forward isn't fully clear, or when people are being asked to stretch beyond what feels comfortable. In schools, where the work is complex and the stakes are high, resistance is part of the work, and it gives you important information about what people need next.

Throughout this book, you've been invited to see resistance differently. Not as defiance or unwillingness, and not as something to push through or manage away. **Resistance is something more useful than that. It's a signal pointing to something that isn't fully supported yet.** That shift changes what you do next.

When resistance gets misread, effort gets misjudged. I've watched incredibly capable educators get labeled as unmotivated, when what was really happening was uncertainty, or overwhelm, or a lack of support in a specific area. Hesitation starts to look like disengagement. Pressure steps in where understanding should have been. And over time, you feel the cost of that. It shows up in the level of trust, energy, and how much people are actually willing to invest.

When resistance is understood, something opens up. You already know this from working with students. When a student struggles to read, we don't label them as resistant and hand them a random strategy. We slow down, listen, and assess what's actually getting in the way. Is it decoding? Fluency? Vocabulary? Comprehension? Then we respond to that. We don't lower expectations, and we don't rush past the struggle. We match the support to the need.

The same thinking applies here. When educators hesitate, disengage, or push back, it's hardly ever about effort or intent. Something underneath is unsupported. When you slow down just enough to figure out what that is, resistance starts to feel different. The work isn't easier, but your response fits, which changes everything.

This is the heart of the human-centered approach to leadership and coaching.

The task-centered approach tends to focus on behaviors, like completion and compliance. It asks, *how do I get people to do the thing?* When resistance shows up, the instinct is to tighten structure, increase pressure, and hope movement follows.

Human-centered leadership starts somewhere else. It asks, *what is this response telling me?* It listens for meaning, safety, confidence, belonging, and agency. It recognizes that engagement is required for sustained action, and that support is what allows accountability to actually work.

When you lead this way, resistance stops feeling like something you have to fight.

You begin to recognize the form it's taking and hear what might be unsupported, which allows you to choose your response with more intention instead of reacting too quickly or jumping straight to a solution. The tools in this book aren't meant to be used all at once or as a protocol. They're there to help you diagnose, decode, and respond in a way that actually fits the moment you're in.

You don't have to hold all of this in your head. Use the Catalyst Mindsets™ Quick Reference when you need it. When resistance shows up, start there. It gives you a place to start and a next step to take. That sequence matters.

When resistance gets met with pressure, engagement shrinks. People comply for a while, then quietly pull back. When it's met with understanding and intentional support, effort has somewhere to go. Conversations open up, ownership starts to build, and you can feel the difference in the room.

This doesn't require perfection. You're still going to misread moments. There will be times you feel that pull to move faster than the situation actually calls for, to skip the pause and go straight to fixing. I still catch myself doing that. It's part of the work.

Your awareness starts to change, and you begin to hear hesitation differently. You notice when pressure is stepping in where clarity should be and you give yourself just enough space to ask a better question instead of reacting to the first one that comes to mind. Those moments can feel small when you're in them, almost easy to overlook, though they're not small at all. The work lives there, and it's what leadership actually looks like in real time.

You don't need more preparation to begin. You don't need the perfect plan or the perfectly worded response. This starts the next time resistance shows up, which it will, probably sooner than you expect. In that moment, what you choose to do next matters more than anything you've read up to this point.

And it's worth saying out loud: Choosing not to respond differently is still a choice.

When resistance goes unexamined, we keep getting the same results. We misread effort, question intent, and add pressure. People start to pull back, even if they're still doing the work.

When resistance is understood, some things start to look different. This isn't about making leadership easier, and it's not about lowering expectations. What changes is how you respond. You start lining up your response with what people actually need to move forward. You stop pushing where pushing doesn't work and meet the moment with more precision.

This book isn't offering quick fixes or neat solutions. It's offering something more practical than that. A way of seeing that changes how you show up. A way of listening that reshapes your next move. A way of leading that builds trust while still protecting the work.

You already have the capacity to do this.

Now you know what to listen for.

Stay attuned to resistance. It's not a dead end. It's a signal. A compass, pointing you toward what needs your attention next.

Follow it.

Bonus Resources

Everything you need, all in one place.

Find all of these resources at:
thewholeeducator.com/book-resources

Overview
Catalyst Mindset Quick Reference

Value Mindset
V.A.L.U.E. Coaching Process

Belonging Mindset
Trust Map
Seeking Questions
Risk Response

Success Mindset
Success Coaching Map

Growth Mindset
Growth Response Tool

Ownership Mindset
Agency Audit

References

Understanding Resistance

Arnsten, A. F. T. (2009). Stress signalling pathways that impair prefrontal cortex structure and function. *Nature Reviews Neuroscience, 10*(6), 410–422. https://doi.org/10.1038/nrn2648

Farrington, C. A. (2013). *Academic mindsets as a critical component of deeper learning.* University of Chicago Consortium on Chicago School Research.

Heifetz, R. A., Kania, J. V., & Kramer, M. R. (2004). Leading boldly. *Stanford Social Innovation Review, 2*(3), 20–32. https://www.issuelab.org/resources/1846/1846.pdf

Hersey, P., Blanchard, K. H., & Natemeyer, W. E. (1979). Situational leadership, perception, and the impact of power. *Group & Organization Studies, 4*(4), 418–428.

Muhammad, A. (2009). *Transforming school culture: How to overcome staff division.* Solution Tree Press.

Oettingen, G., Marquardt, M. K., & Gollwitzer, P. M. (2012). Mental contrasting turns positive feedback on creative potential into successful performance. *Journal of Experimental Social Psychology, 48*(5), 990–996. https://doi.org/10.1016/j.jesp.2012.03.012

Weiner, B. J. (2009). A theory of organizational readiness for change. *Implementation Science, 4*(1), Article 67. https://doi.org/10.1186/1748-5908-4-67

Value Mindset

Eccles, J. S., & Wigfield, A. (2002). Motivational beliefs, values, and goals. *Annual Review of Psychology, 53*, 109–132. https://doi.org/10.1146/annurev.psych.53.100901.135153

Pink, D. H. (2009). *Drive: The surprising truth about what motivates us.* Riverhead Books.

Ryan, R. M., & Deci, E. L. (2000). Intrinsic and extrinsic motivations: Classic definitions and new directions. *Contemporary Educational Psychology, 25*(1), 54–67. https://doi.org/10.1006/ceps.1999.1020

Belonging Mindset

Brown, B. (2018). *Dare to lead: Brave work. Tough conversations. Whole hearts.* Random House.

Covey, S. M. R. (2006). *The speed of trust: The one thing that changes everything.* Free Press.

Duhigg, C. (2024). *Supercommunicators: How to unlock the secret language of connection.* Random House.

Edmondson, A. C. (1999). Psychological safety and learning behavior in work teams. *Administrative Science Quarterly, 44*(2), 350–383. https://doi.org/10.2307/2666999

University of California, San Francisco, & Gallup. (2019). *Belonging: Engagement resource guide.* https://www.gallup.com/workplace/236441/employee-engagement-drives-growth.aspx

Success Mindset

Amabile, T. M., & Kramer, S. J. (2011). The power of small wins. *Harvard Business Review, 89*(5), 70–80.

Artino, A. R., Jr. (2012). Academic self-efficacy: From educational theory to instructional practice. *Perspectives on Medical Education, 1*(2), 76–85. https://doi.org/10.1007/s40037-012-0012-5

Bandura, A. (1977). Self-efficacy: Toward a unifying theory of behavioral change. *Psychological Review, 84*(2), 191–215. https://doi.org/10.1037/0033-295X.84.2.191

Hattie, J., & Timperley, H. (2007). The power of feedback. *Review of Educational Research, 77*(1), 81–112. https://doi.org/10.3102/003465430298487

Lieberman, M. D., Eisenberger, N. I., Crockett, M. J., Tom, S. M., Pfeifer, J. H., & Way, B. M. (2007). Putting feelings into words: Affect labeling disrupts amygdala activity in response to affective stimuli. *Psychological Science, 18*(5), 421–428. https://doi.org/10.1111/j.1467-9280.2007.01916.x

Schunk, D. H., & Pajares, F. (2009). Self-efficacy theory. In K. R. Wentzel & A. Wigfield (Eds.), *Handbook of motivation at school* (pp. 35–53). Routledge.

Tschannen-Moran, M., & Hoy, A. W. (2001). Teacher efficacy: Capturing an elusive construct. *Teaching and Teacher Education, 17*(7), 783–805. https://doi.org/10.1016/S0742-051X(01)00036-1

Weiner, B. (1985). An attributional theory of achievement motivation and emotion. *Psychological Review, 92*(4), 548–573.

Growth Mindset

Briceño, E. (2023). *The performance paradox: Turning the power of mindset into action.* Ballantine Books.

Csikszentmihalyi, M., & Csikszentmihalyi, I. S. (Eds.). (1988). *Optimal experience: Psychological studies of flow in consciousness.* Cambridge University Press.

Dweck, C. S. (2006). *Mindset: The new psychology of success.* Random House.

Dweck, C. S. (2015). Carol Dweck revisits the Growth Mindset. *Education Week, 35*(5), 20–24.

Keating, L. A., & Heslin, P. A. (2015). The potential role of mindsets in unleashing employee engagement. *Human Resource Management Review, 25*(4), 329–341. https://doi.org/10.1016/j.hrmr.2015.01.008

Kegan, R., & Lahey, L. L. (2009). *Immunity to change: How to overcome it and unlock potential in yourself and your organization.* Harvard Business Press.

Ownership Mindset

Bandura, A. (2001). Social cognitive theory: An agentic perspective. *Annual Review of Psychology, 52*(1), 1–26. https://doi.org/10.1146/annurev.psych.52.1.1

Cong-Lem, N. (2021). Teacher agency: A systematic review of international literature. *Issues in Educational Research, 31*(3), 718–738. https://www.iier.org.au/iier31/cong-lem.pdf

du Toit-Brits, C. (2019). Exploring the importance of a sense of belonging for a sense of ownership in learning. *Journal of Educational Studies, 18*(1), 1–15.

Guillot, A., & Collet, C. (2010). Construction of the motor imagery integrative model in sport: A review and theoretical investigation of motor imagery use. International Review of Sport and Exercise Psychology, 3(1), 31–44. https://doi. org/10.1080/17509840903301221

Oettingen, G. (2014). Rethinking positive thinking: Inside the new science of motivation. Current.

Sang, G. (2019). Teacher agency. In M. A. Peters (Ed.), *Encyclopedia of teacher education*. Springer. https://doi. org/10.1007/978-981-13-1179-6_271-1

Saunders, M., Alcantara, V., Cervantes, L., Del Razo, J., López, R., & Perez, W. (2017). *Getting to teacher ownership: How schools are creating meaningful change*. Brown University, Annenberg Institute for School Reform.

Accountability

Latessa, R. A., Galvin, S. L., Swendiman, R. A., Onyango, J., Ostrach, B., Amy C. Edmondson, Davis, S. A., & Hirsh, D. A. (2023). *Psychological safety and accountability in longitudinal integrated clerkships: A dual institution qualitative study*. BMC Medical Education, 23, 760. https://doi.org/10.1186/s12909-023-04622-5

Lencioni, P. (2002). *The five dysfunctions of a team: A leadership fable*. Jossey-Bass.

Locke, E. A., & Latham, G. P. (2002). Building a practically useful theory of goal setting and task motivation: A 35-year odyssey. *American Psychologist, 57*(9), 705–717. https://doi. org/10.1037/0003-066X.57.9.705

Ryan, R. M., & Deci, E. L. (2020). Intrinsic and extrinsic motivation from a self-determination theory perspective: Definitions, theory, practices, and future directions. *Contemporary Educational Psychology, 61*, 101860. https://doi.org/10.1016/j.cedpsych.2020.101860

About the Author

Becca Silver is a global educational speaker, coach, and leadership trainer, and the founder of The Whole Educator. She also hosts the *Coaching the Whole Educator* podcast, which reaches educators in over 100 countries. Her work focuses on helping leaders move beyond compliance and buy-in and respond to resistance with greater understanding, skill, and care.

Becca has spent more than two decades working alongside educators and leaders as they navigate change, pressure, and the human realities of school improvement. Her approach is grounded in transformational learning and a deep understanding of how adults make meaning, shift beliefs, and grow over time. She draws on research in learning science, mindset development, and adult development and translates theory into practical tools leaders can use in real schools, with real constraints.

She has worked alongside researchers in the Growth Mindset field, leading professional learning for schools and districts and helping educators move from awareness of mindset research to meaningful changes in practice. Her work bridges the gap between what the research says and what leaders need to do on Monday morning.

Becca holds a master's degree in Organizational Leadership and Learning with an emphasis on Human Development, as well as a bachelor's degree in Elementary Education. She partners with schools, districts, and education organizations across the United States and internationally, supporting leadership teams when technical solutions are not enough.

She believes resistance is not a failure of people, but a signal of unmet needs. When leaders learn how to read that signal, change stops feeling so hard.